LifeLine
Practical Tools for Everyday Needs
Workbook

Your 10-Day Spiritual Action Plan for
Complete
Financial
Breakthrough

KENNETH
COPELAND
PUBLICATIONS

by Kenneth and Gloria
Copeland

Includes material from the *Believer's Voice of Victory* magazine, *God's Will Is Prosperity, The Laws of Prosperity, Blessed to Be a Blessing* (formerly published as *Managing God's Mutual Funds—Yours and His)*, *One Word From God Can Change Your Finances, Prosperity: The Choice Is Yours, Prosperity Promises,* Kenneth Copeland's Partner Letters, as well as newly created content and interactive action plans inspired by these resources.

Your 10-Day Spiritual Action Plan for Complete Financial Breakthrough

ISBN 978-1-57562-990-2   30-3010

16 15 14 13 12 11   10 9 8 7 6 5

© 2009 Eagle Mountain International Church Inc. aka Kenneth Copeland Ministries

God of Abundance – Praise Series

Let the Lord/No More Bondage/Spirit of the Lord (Medley)
Written by David Ellis; Written by Keith Moore; Written by David Ellis
© 2002 David Ellis / © 1998 Faith Life Publishing

When I Believe/Give (It Shall Be Given Unto You) (Medley)
Written by Clinton Utterbach /Written by Jim Burgdorf
© 1993 Utterbach Music Publishing Co. ASCAP. Administered by Universal-Polygram, Int. Publ. Inc.
ASCAP / © 1996 Macedonia Music. ASCAP

Send Now Prosperity
Written by Michael Howell and David Ellis
© 2002 Kel-Jon Music ASCAP / © 2002 David Ellis

He Set Me Free/Thank You, Father (Medley)
Written by Michael Howell and David Ellis / Written by Keith Moore
© 2002 Kel-Jon Music ASCAP & © 2002 David Ellis / © 1991 Faith Life Publishing

God of Abundance
Written by Len Mink
© 1993 Len Mink Music

I Thank You, Lord
Written by Michael Howell and David Ellis
© 2002 Kel-Jon Music ASCAP & © 2002 David Ellis

More Than Enough
Written by Michael Howell and David Ellis
© 2002 Kel-Jon Music ASCAP & © 2002 David Ellis

I Am Blessed
Written by David Ellis
© 2002 David Ellis

Bread Upon the Water
Written by Bill and Janny Grein
© 1977 Birdwing Music / BMG Songs Inc. / SpiritQuest Music (Admin. by BMG Music Publishing) (Admin. by EMI Christian Music Publishing)

For more information about Kenneth Copeland Ministries, call 800-600-7395 or visit www.kcm.org.

Table of
Contents

How to Use
Your LifeLine Kit

How to Use
Your LifeLine Kit

We believe this *10-Day Spiritual Action Plan for Complete Financial Breakthrough* will change your circumstances. It's our prayer that you experience *true prosperity* like never before—spirit, soul and body. To accomplish this, we've created one of the most in-depth resources Kenneth Copeland Ministries has ever made available on this subject—all in one place. Here are some practical tips to get you started and help you make the most of this kit:

- Commit to making the next 10 days *your* days for renewing your mind. Set aside any distractions and be prepared to make adjustments in your life so you can get the most out of this kit.

- This plan should be a blessing, not a burden. If you miss a day or can't quite get through one day's materials, just start where you left off at your next opportunity. If you have to, be flexible with the kit to ensure you make it to the end. If you only have half an hour a day, that's fine— commit that! It may take longer to complete the kit, but you can be confident those 30 days will still be some of the most life-changing days you've ever had.

- Use this LifeLine workbook as your starting point each day, to guide your reading, listening, watching and journaling. Before you know it, you'll be saturating your life with God's Word like never before.

- We recommend that you:

  > **Read and journal** in the morning 📑🖊
  > **Meditate** on the scriptures daily 🖐
  > **Use** the CD and DVD products daily ⊙
  > as instructed in each chapter
  > **Read and journal** again at night 📑🖊

Remember, the goal is to do a little every day. Steady doses are the best medicine.

- This is an action book! Have a pen handy to underline and take notes.

- Fully engage with all the materials. Write in your workbook, speak the scriptures, pray the prayers, sing with the music and take time to enjoy the materials in every way.

- Carry your daily action card and refer to it throughout your day as a connecting point with God.

- Make your study time focused. Do your best to remove distractions and find a quiet place.

Your Complete Financial Breakthrough is closer than ever! God loves you and He is *for* you. We're standing with you, and remember that "Jesus Is Lord!"

Chapter One
What Is Prosperity?

True Prosperity
by Kenneth Copeland

As we begin this study of prosperity, let me mention that we are putting the Word of God first and foremost throughout this study… not what we *think* it says, but what it *actually* says! When you see truth in the Word, believe it and act on it, your breakthrough *will* come…because when you do these things, faith is created. Romans 10:17 says, "Faith cometh by hearing, and hearing by the word of God."

Let's look at 3 John 2, our foundation scripture. Under the inspiration of the Holy Spirit, the Apostle John wrote, "Beloved, I wish above all things that thou mayest prosper and be in health, even as thy soul prospereth."

Traditionally, the Church has been led to believe that prosperity is bad or ungodly. However, John writes that we *should* prosper and be in health. You see, there is nothing wrong with prosperity, in itself. Contrary to what you may have heard taught, money is *not* the root of all evil. The *love of money* is the root of all evil (1 Timothy 6:10)…and there are people committing that sin who don't have a dime!

So, God has nothing against us being prosperous. In fact, as you will see throughout this study, He *desires* it. Psalm 35:27 says, "Let the Lord be magnified, which hath pleasure in the prosperity of his servant."

You may have picked up this study because you need a financial breakthrough, and I believe it will come as you put these principles to work. But to begin, I want you to realize that true prosperity covers much more than finances.

Elements of True Prosperity

When studying prosperity, you should *never* think of it like the world does, from a carnal viewpoint. You must train yourself to think in line with God's Word. If you're not watchful, when you think of prosperity, all you will see is money—and that's only a *very small* part of prosperity. True prosperity is living in the full understanding and manifestation of THE BLESSING God spoke at Creation when He breathed life, purpose, destiny and abundance of supply into Adam, saying: "Be fruitful, and multiply, and replenish the earth, and subdue it: and have dominion over the fish of the sea, and over the fowl of the air, and over every living thing that moveth upon the earth" (Genesis 1:28). To prosper is to excel, to go to the highest place, in anything desired. True prosperity is allowing God's ability and power to flow through you to meet the needs of mankind—regardless of what those needs may be—spiritually, emotionally, mentally, relationally, financially, or in any other area of life. Those ministered to, in turn, are raised up, strengthened and become powerful. God wants to bring you to that place in His prosperity where THE BLESSING on you and in you creates a Garden of Eden wherever you go.

To the world, prosperity, like everything else, is completely born of the senses or the sense-ruled mind. The world is governed by natural impulses and the physical senses. Its slogan is *seeing is believing.* If you can see it, taste it, hear it, smell it or feel it, then it must be true; if you can't contact it with your physical senses, it is not true.

But the world's definition of prosperity is very limited in scope—it's all about financial ability and power. The world itself admits it has no power to overcome poverty, sickness, spiritual or social ills.

True prosperity is the ability to use God's power to meet the needs of mankind in any realm of life. This covers much more than just finances, politics and society. Money is not the only degree of prosperity. You can have all the money in the world and still be spiritually, mentally and physically poverty stricken. Money is the lowest form of power that exists on earth. Do you know what is the highest? *The power of prayer!* You can pray in the Name of Jesus, and God will use His ability to handle your situation, whatever it is. It takes the power of God to make you completely whole. God's power is the only power that covers the entire spectrum of human existence. God is more than enough!

When you make it your need to get salvation into the hands of people, and make it your purpose to feed the gospel to the unsaved, God will support what you do. This is true prosperity! God has obligated Himself to communicate the message of Jesus Christ to the world. He will move heaven and earth to do it because, to the man who has never heard it, Jesus has never died or been resurrected from the dead. To that man, Jesus' sacrifice means nothing.

The Word says in 1 John 4:17, "...as he is, so are we in this world." When you go to the Lord, He has more than enough to meet your need. Have you ever turned to the Lord with a problem and had Him say, "Well, that's new! You've come up with something heaven can't cover"? Of course not! God has more than enough to solve the worst problem you could have. Jesus is God's channel to us, and we, in turn, are His channel to the world.

True prosperity is the ability to look a man in the eye in his moment of impossibility and take his needs as your own. Those who are spiritual are to help those who are not. We are to bear one another's burdens, and so fulfill the law of Christ" (Galatians 6:2). And when you operate in true prosperity, you'll have more than enough to do just that.

Morning Reflection

What is the root of all evil?

_____
_____
_____
_____
_____

What is the world's definition of prosperity?

_____
_____
_____
_____
_____

What is true prosperity?

_____
_____
_____
_____
_____
_____
_____
_____
_____
_____
_____
_____

Today's Connection Points

⦿ *God of Abundance* CD: "I Am Blessed" (Track 1)

Your breakthrough may seem miles away right now, but as you focus on today's track, consider how much you've been blessed!

⦿ DVD: "Complete Prosperity" (Chapter 1)

Listening to the Word about prosperity will strengthen your faith! Watch as Kenneth talks about how prosperity includes so much more than just finances.

⦿ *Prosperity Scriptures* CD (Track 1)

Deuteronomy 7:13; 1 Chronicles 29:11-12; Psalms 23:1, 35:27, 37:3-5, 25-26, 84:8-12, 85:12, 92:12-15, 115:11-16; Proverbs 8:17-21; Jeremiah 29:11; 3 John 2

Faith in Action

✋ *Realize that God wants you to be prosperous!*
Commit to studying the Word like never before and change your way of thinking.

Notes:

_____
_____
_____
_____
_____
_____
_____
_____
_____
_____
_____
_____
_____
_____
_____
_____
_____
_____
_____
_____
_____
_____
_____

Money Matters

by Gloria Copeland

After reading Ken's Morning Connection, I'm sure you see that true prosperity is about more than just financial blessings. It also includes healing, protection, favor, wisdom, success, well-being and every good thing you could possibly need—all the good things Jesus paid for you to have. Nonetheless, you're going to see that we talk about finances a lot throughout this study.

Why? Because in this day and hour, financial prosperity isn't simply a luxury. It's a *responsibility*. For the committed believer who cares about the eternal destiny of others, money matters.

Money may not seem like a very spiritual issue. You may have been taught that as far as God is concerned, it doesn't matter if you're rich or poor. But I want you to know—it matters. Your not having enough money to finance the gospel won't keep you from going to heaven, but it could keep others from going.

Prosperity is not a frivolous thing with no eternal consequences. It is a serious issue. If you want to know how serious, consider this: Right now, in nations such as the former Soviet Union, there are people who have never heard the gospel. For years, the doors of their nation have been locked to it. But at this moment, the Body of Christ has the opportunity to preach the Word of God from one end of that country to the other.

What will we need to take full advantage of that opportunity? Money.

That's right. Money or the lack of it can determine whether someone in a nation like that hears the gospel...or not. In my eyes, that makes our prosperity as born-again believers an important issue—extremely important.

If we prosper, we'll have enough not just to meet our own little needs, but to send the Word of God around the world. If we don't, we won't. It's that simple.

"Oh, but Gloria, you know we can't *all* be rich."

Yes, we can. Prosperity is not an accident.

It's not a function of circumstances or the economy. According to God's Word, prosperity is a *choice*. It is a personal decision and a spiritual process.

Most people don't know that. Ken and I didn't either, years ago when we first began walking with God. Back then, we were sick some of the time and broke *all* the time. Our life was one financial disaster after another. It felt like we were living under some kind of curse.

Do you know why we felt that way? Because we *were* living under a curse! We just didn't realize it.

Failing to prosper is part of the curse that came upon the earth when Adam sold out to Satan in the Garden of Eden. The curse is described in detail in Deuteronomy 28:15-68 and it includes every kind of sickness, sin, tragedy and lack. That passage says that when you're living under the curse, "You shall be only oppressed and robbed continually.... You shall carry much seed out into the field and shall gather little in" (verses 29, 38, *The Amplified Bible*).

Do you ever feel like that? Every time you try to get ahead, something happens to steal away everything you thought you were going to gain? I know the feeling. I had it for years. But then, one day Ken and I discovered we didn't have to live like that anymore because Jesus has delivered us from the curse. Through His death and resurrection, He has restored to us what Adam lost through sin. He has given back to us the original BLESSING[1] that God gave mankind in the Garden: "Be fruitful, and multiply, and replenish the earth, and subdue it: and have dominion" (Genesis 1:28).

The specific benefits of THE BLESSING (which were passed down by covenant to Abraham and his seed) listed in Deuteronomy 28:1-13, reveal that God has promised great things to us. He has said:

And it shall come to pass, if thou shalt

---

[1]The Lord instructed Ken to emphasize THE BLESSING by using all capital letters when referring to it, so I like to do that too.

hearken diligently unto the voice of the Lord thy God, to observe and to do all his commandments which I command thee this day, that the Lord thy God will set thee on high above all nations of the earth: And all these blessings shall come on thee, and overtake thee, if thou shalt hearken unto the voice of the Lord thy God. Blessed shalt thou be in the city, and blessed shalt thou be in the field. Blessed shall be the fruit of thy body, and the fruit of thy ground, and the fruit of thy cattle, the increase of thy kine, and the flocks of thy sheep. Blessed shall be thy basket and thy store. Blessed shalt thou be when thou comest in, and blessed shalt thou be when thou goest out. The Lord shall cause thine enemies that rise up against thee to be smitten before thy face: they shall come out against thee one way, and flee before thee seven ways. The Lord shall command the blessing upon thee in thy storehouses, and in all that thou settest thine hand unto; and he shall bless thee in the land which the Lord thy God giveth thee. The Lord shall establish thee an holy people unto himself, as he hath sworn unto thee, if thou shalt keep the commandments of the Lord thy God, and walk in his ways (verses 1-9).

Now, does THE BLESSING described there sound too good to be true? Well, it's not. That's THE BLESSING Jesus bought for you on the cross. We'll study it more in depth in coming chapters. For now, just know that it will begin to operate in your life if you'll "hearken diligently unto the voice of the Lord [your] God."

Notice, I didn't say it will operate just because you're a Christian. Ken and I were Christians for five years before we began to listen to God's Word about prosperity. During that time, the curse continued to run loose in our lives. It didn't just creep up quietly. It jumped on us and overtook us. No matter how hard we tried, we couldn't outrun it or get away from it.

Then we began to believe God's Word about prosperity—to be willing and obedient—and good things started to happen. First a few. Then a few more. The longer we obeyed God and walked in faith about finances, the more those good things increased.

Just like the curse once overtook us, now the blessings of God overtake us. I like that much better.

The same thing will happen to you if you'll follow the instructions in Deuteronomy 28:1 because "faith cometh by hearing, and hearing by the word of God" (Romans 10:17). Once faith comes, you can speak to that mountain of financial trouble, command it to be removed, and it will obey you. (See Mark 11:22-24.)

More Than Enough

As you do that, you'll discover, just as Ken and I did, that God doesn't promise just to meet your basic needs, He says He'll give you an abundance. Some religious people would argue about that. But the truth is, there's nothing to argue about because the Word makes it perfectly clear. Look back at what we just read from Deuteronomy 28. It says, "The Lord shall command the blessing upon thee in thy storehouses, and in all that thou settest thine hand unto..." (verse 8).

Look at that for a minute. If you don't have abundance, why would you need a storehouse? A storehouse is where you put the extra, the surplus, the "more-than-enough."

If that's not clear enough, verse 11 says point blank that "the Lord shall make you have a surplus of prosperity" *(The Amplified Bible)*. I want you to remember those words—*a surplus of prosperity*—because that's God's will for you. When you made Jesus Christ the Lord of your life, God's blessing came on you, not so you could just "get by," but so that you could have a surplus of prosperity!

That shouldn't really surprise you. After all, if you look at God's history with man, you'll see that when He had His way, man was abundantly supplied. God has always promised, "If you are willing and obedient, you shall eat the good of the land" (Isaiah 1:19, *The Amplified Bible)*. Understand though, that being willing means more than just saying, "Well, Lord, if You want me to prosper, I'll prosper." Being willing means you apply the force of your will and determine to receive by faith what God has promised, no matter how impossible the circumstances may seem to be.

Start Where You Are

What you need to do is start right where you are. Start believing God for rent money. Start believing God to buy groceries. Start believing, and then increase.

That's what we did. We believed for rent. Then we believed for a car. Then one day we believed for a house. The first time it took us six years to get it. The next time it took three weeks.

The principles you'll learn throughout this study are what Ken and I used to lay our financial foundation, and we use these same principles today to maintain it.

Now, there's no time to waste! We're rapidly coming to the end of this age. Prosperity is not a frivolous matter. It's serious. More hinges on it than you have realized. But if you stand in faith and put the Word you learn here into practice, your financial breakthrough *will* come!

Evening Reflection

Why is money an important matter for today's believer?

_____

_____

_____

_____

What blessings does God promise to the Christian?

_____

_____

_____

_____

What is your part in accepting His promise?

_____

_____

_____

_____

Notes:

_____

_____

_____

_____

_____

_____

_____

_____

_____

_____

_____

_____

_____

_____

_____

_____

_____

Today's Prayer of Faith

Thank You, Father, for giving me prosperity in every area of my life. I commit to listening to Your voice and digging into Your Word. No matter what it looks like right now, I believe I have more than enough! In Jesus' Name. Amen.

Real-Life Testimonies
To Help Build Your Faith

Prosperity Proven

I am a minister but did *not* understand the prosperity message until just a few years ago. I thought it was a "con game" to get people to turn loose of their money. But after watching Kenneth Copeland on TV one day, I was astonished when he said that if he wanted to increase, he wouldn't try to get us to give more, but he would increase his own giving! That was startling to me! After studying what the Bible says about it, God gave me the revelation of this biblical doctrine.

I started partnering with you, and *our* income doubled in 30 days! We now have a nondenominational Bible college where one of the classes I teach is "Principles of Prosperity." I want to thank you for teaching me this truth that I had never heard in church and I believe in it now, wholeheartedly.

Dr. Keith Slough
Kannapolis, N.C.

For practical tools to help you get started on a financial plan, go to kcm.org/financial-tools.

Chapter Two
God's Will Is Prosperity

A Covenant of Prosperity
by Gloria Copeland

God's will concerning financial prosperity and abundance is clearly revealed in the Scriptures. From the beginning of time, He has provided financial prosperity for His people through obedience to His Word.

It started with Adam. In the beginning, God placed everything that man could use and enjoy in the Garden. God saw to it that Adam lacked no good thing. He was created in the image of God, Himself, leaving nothing to be desired.

God furnished Adam with companionship, ability, abundance and a kingdom. He BLESSED Adam with the power to be fruitful, multiply, fill the earth, subdue it and have dominion over every living creature (Genesis 1:28). Adam was the master of the Garden, and God was the master of Adam. God's man was free in every way! He knew no bondage until that fatal day when he committed high treason against the Lord God.

Poverty and lack came only after Adam changed gods and began to operate under Satan's dominion. Satan is the author of poverty. God is the Author of abundance. When Adam served God, all he knew was abundance. He had the best of everything, the crown of life. God's will for Adam was abundance. Since His will does not change, God's will for His people today is still abundance (James 1:17).

The Blessing of Abraham

Once sin entered the picture and robbed man of THE BLESSING and the abundance it brings, God made a way to get that BLESSING back into the earth by establishing a covenant with Abraham (Genesis 17:1-9). It was an unbreakable covenant that could not be altered and, through it, Abraham was blessed physically and materially and given the promise of spiritual redemption.

God's covenant with Abraham revealed His will concerning prosperity because it made Abraham extremely rich. Abraham's servant said, "The Lord has blessed my master abundantly, and he has become wealthy. He has given him sheep and cattle, silver and gold, menservants and maidservants, and camels and donkeys" (Genesis 24:35, *The Amplified Bible*). At the end of Abraham's life, Genesis 24:1 says of him: "And Abraham was old, and well stricken in age: and the Lord had blessed Abraham in all things." No enemy could successfully stand before him because he had a covenant with God. God established the covenant in Abraham's generation, and nothing could alter the promise of God because Abraham kept the covenant and walked uprightly before God.

Abraham's Seed

God promised Abraham that He would also establish His covenant of BLESSING with his seed: "But my covenant will I establish with Isaac" (Genesis 17:21). And that's exactly what He did!

"And the Lord appeared to [Isaac] the same night and said, I am the God of Abraham your father. Fear not, for I am with you and will favor you with blessings and multiply your descendants for the sake of My servant Abraham" (Genesis 26:24, *The Amplified Bible*). The Bible tells us that Isaac "became great and gained more and more until he became very wealthy and distinguished...and the Philistines envied him" (Genesis 26:13-14, *The Amplified Bible*).

Next, God established THE BLESSING in Jacob's life. "Thus the man increased and became exceedingly rich, and had many sheep and goats, and maidservants, menservants, camels, and donkeys" (Genesis 30:43, *The Amplified Bible*). Sound familiar? It's the result of the same covenant. Jacob's father-in-law deceived and cheated him for years, but that could not alter the covenant (Genesis 31:7-12). Jacob said, "...for God has dealt graciously with me and I have everything" (Genesis 33:11, *The Amplified Bible*).

Joseph, Jacob's son, was sold into slavery by his brothers, but that did not stop God from establishing His covenant of BLESSING with

Joseph in his generation. "But the Lord was with Joseph, and he [though a slave] was a successful and prosperous man; and he was in the house of his master the Egyptian. And his master saw that the Lord was with him, and that the Lord made all that he did to flourish and succeed in his hand" (Genesis 39:2-3, *The Amplified Bible*). In short, the Lord made a slave so prosperous that his owner wanted to partake of his success! What a covenant! It works even under the most adverse circumstances.

THE BLESSING of the covenant cannot be stopped in the life of an heir of Abraham as long as he keeps the covenant—obeys God and believes that He is able to perform the covenant in his life.

Later, THE BLESSING prospered Joseph, even in prison. God gave him favor, and the warden put him in charge of the prison. The Lord made whatever Joseph did to prosper (Genesis 39:21-23). Eventually, Joseph was promoted from prison to the office of governor, and given full charge of the country. "And Pharaoh took off his [signet] ring from his hand and put it on Joseph's hand, and arrayed him in [official] vestments of fine linen and put a gold chain about his neck; he made him to ride in the second chariot which he had and [officials] cried before him, Bow the knee! And he set him over all the land of Egypt" (Genesis 41:42-43, *The Amplified Bible*).

Many years later, after Joseph died, the Egyptians made the Israelites their slaves. But, because of THE BLESSING of Abraham, they were delivered. "And God heard their sighing and groaning and [earnestly] remembered His covenant with Abraham, with Isaac, and with Jacob" (Exodus 2:24, *The Amplified Bible*). God told Moses, "And I have come down to deliver them out of the hand and power of the Egyptians and to bring them up out of that land to a land good and large, a land flowing with milk and honey [a land of plenty]" (Exodus 3:8, *The Amplified Bible*). God, Himself, came down to see about Abraham's descendants because of His covenant with him.

An All-Inclusive Promise

God's dealings with Isaac, Jacob, Joseph and Moses were the result of the promise He made to establish the covenant of BLESSING with Abraham's seed in their generations. That BLESSING included *everything* that had to do with their physical, material and financial needs. Healing was included in THE BLESSING. Success and prosperity was included in THE BLESSING—an exceeding financial blessing.

If Abraham's seed in their generations were obedient to the covenant, they walked in THE BLESSING of Abraham. If they were disobedient, they walked in the curse of the law.

The Lord warned them, "Beware lest you say in your [mind and] heart, My power and the might of my hand have gotten me this wealth. But you shall [earnestly] remember the Lord your God for it is He Who gives you power to get wealth, that He may establish His covenant which He swore to your fathers, as it is this day" (Deuteronomy 8:17-18, *The Amplified Bible*).

This scripture reveals some important facts:

1. God has given covenant men the power to get wealth.

2. Prosperity, even wealth, is necessary to establish the covenant.

3. In order for God to fulfill what He promised Abraham, He must be allowed to prosper Abraham's descendants as it is this day—as though today were the day He made the promise.

In the next session we're going to see how, in Christ, *we* too, are the covenant descendants of Abraham (Galatians 3:29). We're going to see how Jesus made it possible for you and me to receive THE BLESSING of Abraham. The old covenant was incomplete as far as man's needs were concerned. It could not change men's hearts; it could only bless them physically and materially (Galatians 3:21). The new covenant, ratified by the blood of Jesus, was the fulfillment of God's promise to Abraham. It is a better covenant, and rests on better promises (Hebrews 8:6).

The men we've studied prove God's will concerning prosperity. Under their covenant, they were exceedingly wealthy. They lived to be old and died satisfied (Genesis 25:8, 35:29). Whatever they did prospered as long as they were upright before the Lord. God's will is prosperity!

Morning
Reflection

What was the financial result of the covenant God made with Abraham?

_____

_____

_____

_____

How did that covenant affect Abraham's descendants?

_____

_____

_____

_____

How does the covenant affect your life as a Christian?

_____

_____

_____

_____

Today's
Connection Points

⊙ *God of Abundance* CD: "Send Now Prosperity" (Track 2)

Your *complete* prosperity is God's will. Celebrate this truth with today's worship track.

⊙ DVD: "Creating the Garden" (Chapter 2)

Discover the power of THE BLESSING and how God wants to create the Garden of Eden in every area of *your* life.

⊙ *Prosperity Scriptures* CD (Track 2)

Leviticus 26:3-5; Deuteronomy 6:1-3; Joshua 1:7-8; 1 Kings 2:3; Job 36:11; Psalm 1:1-3; Proverbs 3:9-10, 13:11-13, 19:17; Isaiah 58:10-11; Jeremiah 17:7-8; Malachi 3:10-12; 2 Corinthians 9:6-7; Galatians 6:6-10; Hebrews 11:6

Faith in Action

✋ ***Challenge the traditions you've been taught about prosperity.***

God delights in your financial well-being!

Notes:

_____

_____

_____

_____

_____

_____

_____

_____

_____

_____

_____

_____

_____

_____

_____

_____

_____

_____

_____

_____

_____

_____

_____

_____

_____

_____

_____

_____

_____

_____

_____

_____

_____

_____

_____

_____

_____

_____

_____

_____

_____

_____

The Whole Gospel
by Kenneth Copeland

God's will is that we live prosperous lives. The principles in the Word, including the principles of prosperity, are not just for our spirits; they are also for our minds and bodies. As the Church, we seem to have missed the fact that Jesus came to bring this gospel to free us completely—and that includes our financial freedom. That's the *whole gospel.*

Look at Luke 4:16-21 for proof of this:

And [Jesus] came to Nazareth, where he had been brought up: and, as his custom was, he went into the synagogue on the sabbath day, and stood up for to read. And there was delivered unto him the book of the prophet Esaias. And when he had opened the book, he found the place where it was written, The Spirit of the Lord is upon me, because he hath anointed me to preach the gospel to the poor; he hath sent me to heal the brokenhearted, to preach deliverance to the captives, and recovering of sight to the blind, to set at liberty them that are bruised, to preach the acceptable year of the Lord. And he closed the book, and he gave it again to the minister, and sat down. And the eyes of all them that were in the synagogue were fastened on him. And he began to say unto them, This day is this scripture fulfilled in your ears.

In the light of this scripture, the gospel has never been preached to the poor. I'm not talking about the new birth. I'm talking about each of the categories Jesus mentioned in these scriptures.

He was anointed to preach. To the captives, He preached deliverance. To the brokenhearted, He preached healing. To the blind, He preached recovery of sight. He outlined here that the gospel covers many areas. We have preached healing, recovering of sight, deliverance and the new birth to the poor; but we have never preached *the gospel* to the poor.

The Gospel to the Poor

What is the gospel to the poor? The gospel to the poor is that Jesus has come and they don't have to be poor anymore! Prosperity is His will for them! Not very many poverty-stricken people have ever heard the whole gospel. Most of them have heard that they are supposed to live a meager existence. That is what the missionaries who preached to them believed.

There are always some missionaries who will become upset and argue, "You can preach abundance in the United States, but don't come to Africa and preach it." Or, they tell me, "It won't work in El Salvador." "It won't work in Nicaragua," etc.

But when you are preaching the Word of God, it *works.* God could care less whether anyone listening has a dime or not. He didn't base His gospel on what government happens to be in power at the time. All God is looking for is *faith.* There is enough undiscovered wealth in the poorest nations to turn their poverty into abundance if they would just believe the gospel. Even if there weren't, God is more than able to put it there.

God is not limited by what part of the world you live in or what government you live under. Believers all over the world have proven this fact. I've heard testimonies of God prospering people in the most devastated places like Africa, El Salvador, Nicaragua and South America. The laws that govern abundance work for anyone who will put them to work. We need to stop allowing poverty-stricken people to believe that staying poor will somehow make them more pious and sanctified. If this were true, the people of today's starving Third World nations would be holy right now!

The Reason For Prosperity

The Body of Christ must know this about prosperity: It is God's will. He desires to prosper His people. People have the idea that spiritual things are separate from material things. That isn't true. Spiritual laws govern material things. A Spirit created all matter. So the laws of prosperity will work for anyone who will meet the biblical requirements to walk in them.

And why does God want us to prosper? The Word says, "Let him that stole steal no more: but rather let him labour, working with his hands the thing which is good, that he may have to give to him that needeth" (Ephesians 4:28). The whole purpose for gainful employment and prosperity is to take God's laws and prosper by them, and then do something about the poverty in the rest of the world.

Some rich people don't want to do anything but stay rich. But if I reach out and preach the gospel to a born-again man from Mozambique, he has some hope for the first time in his life. He learns that God wants to prosper him and his people. To the starving man that doesn't mean a

Cadillac! It means that God will show him how to get some rain on his scorched ground. God will do something about the poisons in his land, so he can grow good crops and feed his family.

The gospel not only gives him hope in the kingdom to come, but through Jesus and the message that God wants to prosper His people, it gives him hope in the here and now! God intended for material creation to bless and prosper His people.

We can't solve the world's problems with our natural, limited minds, but if we'll allow God to illuminate our human consciousness with His way of thinking, nothing is impossible.

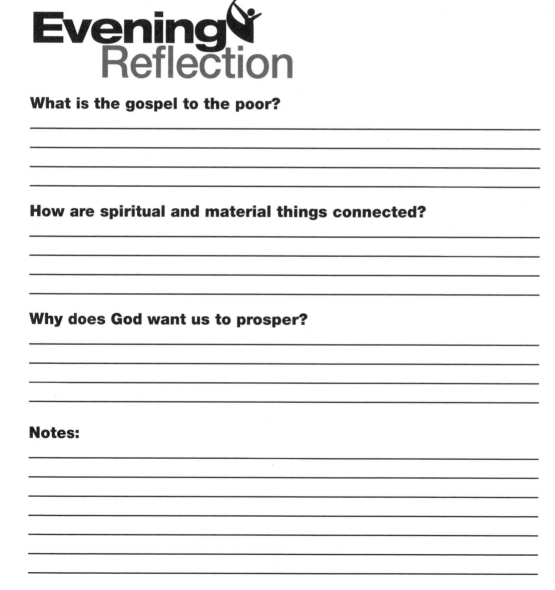

Evening Reflection

What is the gospel to the poor?

_____

_____

_____

_____

How are spiritual and material things connected?

_____

_____

_____

_____

Why does God want us to prosper?

_____

_____

_____

_____

Notes:

_____

_____

_____

_____

_____

_____

_____

_____
_____
_____
_____
_____
_____
_____
_____
_____
_____
_____
_____

Today's
Prayer of Faith

Father, I see that it is Your will that I prosper. Thank You for prospering me so I may bless the poor around me, bringing them hope and good news. In Jesus' Name. Amen.

Real-Life Testimonies
To Help Build Your Faith

Abundant Harvest Time

I just wanted to tell you that your teachings have transformed our lives in the area of finances. We applied principles you've taught us, and have seen an awesome move of God. I can't tell you all of it here—it is too much! But we went from living week to week, to living debt free, and now we are building a brand-new home. When we finish it, it will be debt free. We just purchased two new vehicles and paid cash. This happened in a very short time.

We took your teachings about planting and speaking what we wanted and not what we had. We have planted like that for about 14 years and now God is pouring out a blessing that we cannot contain. When our harvest started coming in, it came like a flood…. My husband's business started prospering more than it ever had. It was a mighty move of God. Thank you for your teachings. God is moving. This year has truly been a year of overflow in our lives.

P.J.
Alabama

For practical tools to help you get started on a financial plan, go to
kcm.org/financial-tools.

Chapter Three
Prosperity Is Our Inheritance

Receive Your Inheritance
by Gloria Copeland

Have you ever been invited to an attorney's office for the reading of a will?

I haven't. Where I come from, there was never enough money left for the relatives to fight over when somebody died. Most of the people I knew didn't leave wills...they left bills.

But, glory to God, that's not the case anymore. I became heir to a fortune, more than 40 years ago in Little Rock, Arkansas, when I gave my life to Jesus. At that moment, I was born again into the richest family ever known. I was born into the royal family that owns and operates the universe. I received an inheritance so vast, it will take me eternity to fully comprehend it.

Some people get excited about tracing their natural family history. They like to know if they have great people in their family tree because it makes them feel they come from good stock. You and I ought to be that way about our heritage as believers. Our ancestors are the greatest men and women who ever walked the face of the earth. We can trace our lineage back to Abraham, Isaac, Jacob, Joseph, King David... all the way to Jesus. Think about that! Those are our forefathers.

"Now wait a minute," you may say. "Those are Jewish men. They lived in Canaan and Israel. You're an American from Arkansas! You're not part of that family."

Well, not physically. But spiritually, according to the Bible, yes, I am. And if you've made Jesus Christ the Lord of your life, you are, too, because Galatians 3 says:

Christ hath redeemed us from the curse of the law, being made a curse for us: for it is written, Cursed is every one that hangeth on a tree: That the blessing of Abraham might come on the Gentiles through Jesus Christ; that we might receive the promise of the Spirit through faith.... And if ye be Christ's, then are ye Abraham's seed, and heirs according to the promise (verses 13-14, 29).

Let's Read the Will

As a Christian, you are the seed of Abraham! What does that mean? It means everything God promised him—everything we read about in the last session—belongs to you. It has been passed down to you, through Jesus.

Abraham's blessing is your inheritance! It has been willed to you by the Word of God. So let's read the will today. Let's look again and find out how God treated Abraham, because that's how God has promised to treat us.

Genesis 12 is a good place to start. There, we see the first promise God made to Abraham: "I will make of thee a great nation, and I will bless thee, and make thy name great; and thou shalt be a blessing: And I will bless them that bless thee, and curse him that curseth thee: and in thee shall all families of the earth be blessed" (verses 2-3).

To fully grasp what God was saying here, you must realize that when He blesses someone, He is not just telling them to have a good day. He is conferring upon them the power to increase and prosper in every area of life. In fact, according to W.E. Vine and Webster's dictionary, the true definition of *bless* is "to cause to prosper, to make happy, to bestow favor upon, to consecrate to holy purposes, to make successful, to make prosperous in temporal concerns pertaining to this life, to guard and preserve."

It was actually THE BLESSING of God that made Abraham rich! It caused him to prosper wherever he went.

Put Your Name in the Promise

Years ago, when Ken and I first started to walk with the Lord, we were facing debts and problems that seemed overwhelming. So I took God's promise to Abraham and put my name in it. I decided that since I was an heir of Abraham, those words were just as true for me as they were for him. And sure enough, they have been. In the years since, God has rewarded me beyond anything I could ask or think. He has been as faithful to me as He was to Abraham!

God keeps His promises, and He promised Abraham that He would bless His seed. He said, "I will make thee exceeding fruitful, and I will make nations of thee, and kings shall come out of thee. And I will establish my covenant between me and thee and thy seed after thee in their generations for an everlasting covenant, to be a God unto thee, and to thy seed after thee" (Genesis 17:6-7).

Circumstances Can't Stop
THE BLESSING

When I look at the life of Abraham, I'm convinced there is no limit to what THE BLESSING of God can do for those who dare to believe. It makes the impossible possible! It will enable you to prosper no matter what's happening around you. It will cause you to increase in the midst of recessions, depressions, and every other kind of economic calamity the devil can dream up.

If you're the seed of Abraham, you shouldn't even worry about such things. They don't have to affect you. You're not dependent on the economic cycles of this natural realm. You're not dependent on what the Federal Reserve does. You are dependent on your covenant with Almighty God—and that never changes! He never alters the Word that comes out of His mouth, and He has said you are BLESSED!

What's more, He's said you're a blessing. That means the company or corporation you work for will be blessed just because you're there.

You've Inherited It All!

As we read last session, Abraham, Isaac, Joseph and others each had quite a success story, but you should have an even better one. You are an heir, not only of the same covenant they had, but of a better one with even better promises (Hebrews 8:6). Available to you are all the natural blessings Abraham, Isaac and Joseph enjoyed, plus the spiritual blessings Jesus won for you when He died on the cross and rose again.

God wanted you to be so sure of that, He gave you a double guarantee. He not only gave His promise, He backed it with an oath:

For when God made [His] promise to Abraham, He swore by Himself, since He had no one greater by whom to swear, saying, Blessing I certainly will bless you and multiplying I will multiply you.... Accordingly God also, in His desire to show more convincingly and beyond doubt to those who were to inherit the promise the unchangeableness of His purpose and plan, intervened...with an oath. This was so that, by two unchangeable things [His promise and His oath] in which it is impossible for God ever to prove false or deceive us, we who have fled [to Him] for refuge might have mighty indwelling strength and strong encouragement to grasp and hold fast the hope appointed for us.... [Now] we have this [hope] as a sure and steadfast anchor of the soul... (Hebrews 6:13-14, 17-19, *The Amplified Bible).*

Yes, that should be an anchor for your soul! When Satan comes to you and says, "You won't make it. You'll never prosper. You'll never have a good job. You'll never have that home you need," God's promise and oath ought to rise up within you. You ought to say, "I am an heir. I have inherited a promise that God will bless me and multiply me. Now get out of here devil, you're not going to get my inheritance!"

Faith Opens the Door

You may not feel very blessed right now. You may not look very blessed. When you check the balance in your bank account, it may not appear that you are heir to anything. Naturally speaking, your situation may seem absolutely hopeless.

If so, remember you're in good company. Abraham once faced similar hopelessness. When God first promised him he'd have a son, he and Sarah both were old and wrinkled. They'd tried for years, without success, to have a baby.

But Abraham, "[human reason for] hope being gone, hoped in faith that he should become the father of many nations, as he had been promised..." (Romans 4:18, *The Amplified Bible).*

Abraham believed God when there was no hope. He believed even when the world said, "It's impossible." "And being not weak in faith... he staggered not at the promise of God through unbelief; but was strong in faith, giving glory to God; and being fully persuaded that, what he had promised, he was able also to perform" (Romans 4:19-21).

THE BLESSING of Abraham comes to us when we do what he did. It comes to us when we believe God's Word. As Romans 5:2 says, "we have access by faith into this grace...."

Faith gives us access to the favor and grace of God, and it gives God access to our lives. It opens the door to our inheritance. And since faith comes by hearing, and hearing by the Word of God, I suggest you get out your Bible.

Start reading it with a new perspective, not like a book of stories, but as the record of your

forefathers. Read and believe it like you would a will that details your inheritance and you will begin to enjoy the riches that are yours by virtue of the new birth.

You'll discover for yourself that you are truly an heir to the limitless resources of the family of God!

Morning Reflection

What does it mean to be the seed of Abraham?

_____
_____
_____
_____

What is the hope we have that is an "anchor" to our soul?

_____
_____
_____
_____

What part does faith play in receiving the blessings of God?

_____
_____
_____
_____

Today's Connection Points

- **God of Abundance CD: "He Set Me Free/Thank You, Father, for Meeting My Needs (Medley)" (Track 3)**

  You are heir to THE BLESSING! Proclaim your freedom from the curse, today.

- **DVD: "Removing the Curse" (Chapter 3)**

  Watch as Kenneth talks about how THE BLESSING removes the curse of lack from our lives.

- **Prosperity Scriptures CD (Track 3)**

  Genesis 13:2, 5-6, 14-17, 17:1-9; Deuteronomy 8:17-18, 28:1-14; Psalm 112:1-4, 132:12-18; Hebrews 7:19-22, 8:6

Faith
in Action

🖐 **You are heir to THE BLESSING!**

Read Deuteronomy 28:1-14, inserting your own name in the scriptures, and declare the many blessings that are yours through Christ (Galatians 3:13-14).

Notes:

_____
_____
_____
_____
_____
_____
_____
_____
_____
_____
_____
_____
_____
_____
_____
_____
_____
_____
_____
_____
_____
_____
_____
_____
_____
_____
_____
_____
_____
_____
_____
_____
_____
_____
_____
_____
_____
_____
_____
_____
_____
_____
_____

A Blessing or a Curse?
by Kenneth Copeland

As we study THE BLESSING and the curse in scripture, I want to address something: Some people have the idea that to prosper financially is a curse. Others believe that if God were to bless them, He would do it by making them poor. I want us to determine from God's Word whether prosperity is a blessing or a curse. And I want us to see the difference between the two. Once we do that, we can forever establish the direction God wants us to take in the financial realm.

Our scriptural basis is Deuteronomy 30:19-20:

> I call heaven and earth to record this day against you, that I have set before you life and death, blessing and cursing: therefore choose life, that both thou and thy seed may live: that thou mayest love the Lord thy God, and that thou mayest obey his voice, and that thou mayest cleave unto him: for he is thy life, and the length of thy days: that thou mayest dwell in the land which the Lord sware unto thy fathers, to Abraham, to Isaac, and to Jacob, to give them.

This promise applies to the New Testament believer because the covenant was made with Abraham *and his seed.* Galatians 3:29 tells us that if we are Christ's, we are Abraham's seed.

Notice that *we* are the ones who must choose. God will not make the decision for us. If we don't choose life, cursing will automatically come on us. It will be our fault, not God's.

The Curse of the Law

Since we must choose, we need to know if prosperity is a blessing or a curse. Deuteronomy 28:15 says, "It shall come to pass, if thou wilt not hearken unto the voice of the Lord thy God, to observe to do all his commandments and his statutes which I command thee this day; that all these curses shall come upon thee, and overtake thee." He is about to list some *curses,* not blessings.

Verses 16-17 say, "Cursed shalt thou be in the city, and cursed shalt thou be in the field. Cursed shall be thy basket and thy store." Your basket and store point directly to the area of finances, or lack of them.

Verse 18 says, "Cursed shall be the fruit of thy body, and the fruit of thy land, the increase of thy kine, and the flocks of thy sheep." Fruit is born or brought into being. Fruit is increase. This verse is talking about family increase as well as the flourishing of material assets.

To curse the increase means that there will not be any increase. Note that the purpose of the cursed increase was not to teach a spiritual lesson—it was to destroy! This chapter says that the curse comes to destroy until you perish. That's certainly no blessing.

Notice verse 20: "The Lord shall send upon thee cursing, vexation, and rebuke...." The verb tense in the original Hebrew indicates that God actually has nothing to do with sending these. These Hebrew verbs are permissive. God will allow these things to come. Once He has delegated authority, God cannot do anything else but permit them. Those who have dominion over the destruction and the curse are responsible for exercising that dominion.

God is not protecting us from the devil. As far as He is concerned, Satan has been defeated and the Body of Christ has been given authority over the evil one. This is true concerning finances as well. Poverty is a curse and the Bible says we have been redeemed from it.

Let's continue with verse 31: "Thine ox shall be slain before thine eyes, and thou shalt not eat thereof: thine ass (or, in today's terms, 'thy car') shall be violently taken away from before thy face, and shall not be restored to thee: thy sheep shall be given unto thine enemies, and thou shalt have none to rescue them." To lose everything—your job, your assets and your possessions—without any way to get them back, is a *curse.*

Poverty destroys. It goes around like an armed robber. God calls lack a curse, so there is no way it could ever be a blessing.

Jesus came to minister to the poor. Why? To make them poorer? Of course not! The Bible says He became poor that we might become rich (2 Corinthians 8:9). He bore the curse of poverty in order to get us out of it—not to leave us in it.

THE BLESSING of Abraham

"Christ hath redeemed us from the curse of the law, being made a curse for us: for it is written, Cursed is every one that hangeth on a tree: That THE BLESSING of Abraham might come on the Gentiles through Jesus Christ; that we might receive the promise of the Spirit through faith" (Galatians 3:13-14).

Remember, God has given us a choice. Let's go back to Deuteronomy 28 and see what a blessing is, so that we will know what to choose.

Verses 1-2 say, "And it shall come to pass, if thou shalt hearken diligently unto the voice of the Lord thy God, to observe and to do all his commandments which I command thee this day, that the Lord thy God will set thee on high above all nations of the earth: And all these blessings shall come on thee, and overtake thee...."

Look at verse 4: "Blessed shall be the fruit of thy body, and the fruit of thy ground, and the fruit of thy cattle, the increase of thy kine, and the flocks of thy sheep." Obviously, increase is a blessing.

Verse 8: "The Lord shall command the blessing upon thee in thy storehouses, and in all that thou settest thine hand unto; and he shall bless thee in the land which the Lord thy God giveth thee." God wants to increase His people.

The Reason for THE BLESSING

Now, remember, God doesn't prosper us financially just so we can be more comfortable. He doesn't heal us so we can watch television without pain in our bodies.

Wealth is not to provide more conveniences and luxuries. Without the Word directing our lives, that's exactly what will happen. This has been a major problem in the Body of Christ as prosperity has been preached. A great number of people in the Body use the increase of God just to become more comfortable. I've been guilty of it myself, but thank God I've repented. I believe the Body of Christ is beginning to wake up. We're beginning to use our increase to win the world instead of increasing our own goods. God wants you to prosper, not just to put food on your table, but also to reach out and help provide food for someone else. Prosperity enables you to be about your Father's business—meeting the needs of others, spirit, soul and body. If you give, it will be given to you. As you seek first the kingdom of God—to reach out to others as Jesus reached out—God will supernaturally meet your needs.

Change your image today. Begin seeing yourself as the one who takes his eyes off of himself and looks to the needs of others (Ephesians 4:28). Prosperity is a blessing for the world. Walk in that revelation today! It is your inheritance. Choose life and blessing, and see the miraculous take place right in your own home!

Evening Reflection

What happens if we don't *choose* to live in God's blessings?

_____

_____

_____

_____

_____

_____

_____

_____

_____

List some differences between THE BLESSING and the curse.

_____
_____
_____
_____

Why does God bless His people?

_____
_____
_____
_____

Notes:

_____
_____
_____
_____
_____
_____
_____
_____
_____
_____
_____
_____
_____
_____
_____
_____
_____
_____
_____
_____
_____
_____
_____
_____
_____
_____
_____
_____
_____
_____
_____
_____

Today's
Prayer of Faith

Father, I thank You that I am an heir to THE BLESSING! I choose life today. I choose to be a conduit for what You want to do in this world. Thank You for Your Word and the many blessings that are mine. In Jesus' Name. Amen.

Real-Life Testimonies
To Help Build Your Faith

Crippling Debt Is Broken

I recently wrote to you asking for your prayers that I may be set free from a crippling debt I was in. You replied to me through a letter in which you encouraged me to be in agreement with you according to Matthew 18:19-20. Praise God, today I am completely free.

I never knew how good it is to be out of debt. Now I am able to get paid, pay my tithes, offerings and discuss with my wife how to spend all the other remaining balance. This is very new to us and it has really brought a lot of peace and love in our marriage.

May my sovereign Lord bless you abundantly, as your candle gives light to our candle. God bless you.

S.M.
Zimbabwe

For practical tools to help you get started on a financial plan, go to kcm.org/financial-tools.

Chapter Four
The Truth About Tithing

The Tithe—Is It for Today?

by Kenneth Copeland

When it comes to living a prosperous life, tithing—giving the first 10 percent of your income to God—is the first subject that must be discussed because it is the cornerstone of real, biblical prosperity. God's financial blessings are reserved for the tither alone. The person who fails to tithe disqualifies himself from receiving his inheritance of abundance.

I realize those words sound stern, but I'm not the one who originated them. God, Himself, said them in Malachi 3:8: "Will a man rob God? Yet ye have robbed me. But ye say, Wherein have we robbed thee? In tithes and offerings."

You see, according to the Bible, the first 10 percent of our income does not belong to us. It belongs to God. He owns it. If we use it on ourselves, we've stolen it from Him.

It amazes me how many believers waste their energies arguing whether or not tithing is a New Testament doctrine. I've heard people say, "Tithing is under the Law! We're not under the Law of Moses, we're under grace. That's why I don't tithe. Oh, I give offerings, but I don't tithe." People who think this way are self-deceived.

Tithing didn't begin with the Law! According to Genesis 4:2-4, before the Law was ever given to Moses, Abel and Cain brought the firstfruits of their labor to God.

Again in Genesis 14, we find that Abraham tithed—before the Law! Abraham and 318 of his armed servants had conquered a group of enemy kings, slaughtered them and took the spoils. And the very first thing he did was tithe the spoils. Melchizedek, the priest, blessed Abraham and said, "Blessed be Abram of the most high God, possessor of heaven and earth: And blessed be the most high God, which hath delivered thine enemies into thy hand. And he gave him tithes of all" (verses 19-20). So tithing didn't begin with the Law. The Law only explained the tithe, gave it procedure and demanded it.

The New Covenant

But, is tithing under the new covenant as well? To answer this question, let's first read Hebrews 7:1-8:

> For this Melchisedec, king of Salem, priest of the most high God, who met Abraham returning from the slaughter of the kings, and blessed him; to whom also Abraham gave a tenth part of all; first being by interpretation King of righteousness, and after that also King of Salem, which is, King of peace; without father, without mother, without descent, having neither beginning of days, nor end of life; but made like unto the Son of God; abideth a priest continually. Now consider how great this man was, unto whom even the patriarch Abraham gave the tenth of the spoils. And verily they that are of the sons of Levi, who receive the office of the priesthood, have a commandment to take tithes of the people according to the law, that is, of their brethren, though they come out of the loins of Abraham: But he whose descent is not counted from them received tithes of Abraham, and blessed him that had the promises. And without all contradiction the less is blessed of the better. And here men that die receive tithes; but there he receiveth them, of whom it is witnessed that he liveth.

What do these verses mean? Simply, that Melchizedek was a man whose birth was not on record. His genealogy could not be traced back to Levi (or the tribe of the priesthood). Nevertheless Melchizedek was made a priest by God and received Abraham's tithes. You cannot argue that tithing is just under the Law because this happened 400 years *before* the Law!

Hebrews 5:6 tells us that Jesus is a High Priest after the order of Melchizedek. He has all the rights that Melchizedek had, which included the right to bless the tithe. Under the new covenant, Jesus not only receives our tithes, He blesses them and then blesses us just as Abraham was blessed. Why? Because as Galatians 3:14 says, "The blessing of Abraham [has] come on the Gentiles through Jesus Christ!" The day that Melchizedek blessed Abraham, that very blessing was handed to you and me through Jesus Christ—our High Priest after the order of Melchizedek! If Melchizedek blessed Abraham, then how much more will Jesus bless us!

Tithing activates THE BLESSING of God in our finances. Read Malachi 3:10-12:

> Bring ye all the tithes into the store-house, that there may be meat in mine house, and prove me now herewith, saith the Lord of hosts, if I will not open you the windows of heaven, and pour you out a blessing, that there shall not be room enough to receive it. And I will rebuke the devourer for your sakes, and he shall not destroy the fruits of your ground; neither shall your vine cast her fruit before the time in the field, saith the Lord of hosts. And all nations shall call you blessed: for ye shall be a delight-some land, saith the Lord of hosts.

God promises that when you tithe, He'll rebuke the devil and command him to keep his hands off your finances. And that promise is as good today as it ever was because when God re-bukes the devil, he stays rebuked!

Common Mistakes

If you're just getting started, let me help you avoid some of the mistakes I often see Christians make in this area of tithing.

For instance, some have come to me and said, "Brother Copeland, I'm using my tithe money to buy preaching CDs. I need to hear them."

That is not a valid use for tithe money. It is not to be spent on yourself, no matter how good the purpose might seem.

Also, God instructs us to "bring ye all the tithes into the storehouse, that there may be meat in mine house..." (Malachi 3:10). That means He intends for you to put your tithe into a place that feeds you spiritually. Usually that will be your local church. Your tithe belongs to Jesus alone. He's the One to whom you tithe, and He is the only One who has any right to tell you where that tithe should go. So, you need to spend some time with Him on your knees, and let Him show you by His Spirit and by His Word exactly what He wants you to do with His 10 percent. If every believer in the Body of Christ would do that, there would be more than enough for every God-ordained ministry. The pastor would have plenty. The evangelist would have plenty. The teacher would have plenty. Everyone would be supplied.

Another mistake people sometimes make is neglecting to separate that first 10 percent from the rest of their income. "After all," they say, "it all belongs to God, and we know we'll end up giving more than 10 percent anyway."

That's wrong. Your money isn't "all God's." He gave 90 percent of it to you. It's yours to enjoy and to use for offerings. The first 10 percent, however, *is* God's and He expects it to be divided out as such with respect and rever-ence to Him.

Notice I said the *first* 10 percent. God is to come first—before your bills, before your savings, even before your taxes. You see, if you don't tithe on your gross income, you're putting the government before God. You're excluding Him from that portion of your income and it won't be blessed.

Yes, tithing is part of the new covenant. Don't wait until your back is against the wall be-fore you use your faith and begin tithing. Learn to act on the Word now, and when Satan tries to pin you against the wall, you can smile and know that you have it made.

Morning Reflection

What is the tithe?

_____
_____
_____
_____

When did the tithe begin?

_____
_____
_____
_____

When should you start tithing?

_____
_____
_____
_____

Today's Connection Points

● *God of Abundance* **CD: "Bread Upon the Water" (Track 4)**

As you keep casting your bread upon the water, it will come back home on every wave!

● **DVD: There is no DVD teaching today.**

● *Prosperity Scriptures* **CD (Track 4)**

2 Chronicles 1:12; Proverbs 2:6-7, 3:13-18, 4:7-9; Ecclesiastes 2:26; 1 Corinthians 1:30; James 1:5, 3:17

Faith in Action

Give your tithe—the first 10 percent of your income— faithfully, with a grateful heart.

Notes:

10% of Your Income...
100% of Your Heart

by Gloria Copeland

Jesus is coming back soon! We don't have time to sit around wishing we had enough money to go through the doors God is opening before us. We don't have time to say, "Well, one day when finances aren't so tight, I'll give to this ministry or that one, so they can buy television time in Russia or print books in Spanish." We need to increase so we can give—and we need to do it now!

How do we get on that road to increase? I can tell you in two simple words: *through tithing.* In the plan of God, *tithing* and *wealth* are so closely connected that in the Hebrew language, they both come from the same root word.

Tithing is the covenant transaction that opens the door for God to be directly involved in our increase. It is a two-way exchange in which we honor God by giving Him 10 percent of our income and He, in return, provides us with a "surplus of prosperity" (Deuteronomy 28:11, *The Amplified Bible).* You can read again how that transaction works in Malachi 3:10-12.

More Than a Religious Routine

"But Gloria," you may say, "I know Christians who have been tithing for years and they're not wealthy!"

Actually, you don't. You just know people who have put 10 percent of their income into the offering bucket. They went through the motions, but they weren't really tithing. We've all done that, at times.

You see, tithing isn't just a matter of the pocketbook. It is a matter of the heart. That's the way it is with everything as far as God is concerned. He *always* looks on the heart. So when we tithe as a religious routine, not in faith, just because we're supposed to and not as a genuine expression of our love for God, we miss out on the blessings of it.

That's what happened to the people in Malachi's day. They were bringing sacrifices to the Lord. They were going through the motions of tithing. But they were not being blessed. In fact, they were living under a financial curse because the attitude of their heart was not right.

In Malachi 1:6-8 the Lord said what was missing from the tithes and offerings of the people was *honor.* They weren't giving God their best. Because they didn't love and reverence God in their hearts, they were offering Him their leftovers. They were fulfilling religious requirements by keeping a formula with no worship.

As tithers, we should learn a lesson from them. When we find ourselves suffering financial lack and failing to enjoy the supernatural increase God has promised, we should check our attitude—*fast!* We should make sure we're giving God our best (not our leftovers) and honoring Him with all our hearts.

Don't Forget Faith

When you really understand what a great deal tithing is, you'll have a hard time *not* getting excited about it! You'll want to jump and shout and praise God every time you think about it. You won't begrudge God His 10 percent, you'll thank Him for letting it flow through your hands.

He didn't have to do that, you know. He could have just given us the 90 percent and withheld the 10, or He could have withheld 90 and given us 10! But He didn't. He gave it to us so we could use it to keep the door of prosperity open. He gave it to us so we could return it and establish a covenant of blessing with Him.

Do you realize what a wonderful privilege it is to have a financial covenant with Almighty God? Do you understand what it means to be connected to His heavenly economy?

It means we don't have to worry about depression or recession—there is no recession or depression in heaven. It means we can sleep peacefully at night when the rest of the world is tormented by fear of financial failure. It means when the devil comes to steal our increase, we can stand firmly on that covenant and say, "Get out of here, Satan! We're tithers and the Word of God says you cannot devour our money. You can't devour our children. You can't devour our health. We've given God the firstfruits of all our increase so we are blessed. And what God has blessed, you can't curse!"

"Lord...Bless Me!"

The fact is, God has already treated us with overwhelming kindness. He has already given us all more than we ever dreamed possible. He has saved us. He has provided healing for us. He has blessed us in a thousand different ways. And that's what we should remember every time we tithe. We should come before the Lord and thank Him for bringing us into our promised land. Tithe with an attitude of gratitude.

If you'll read Deuteronomy 26, you'll see that's what God instructed the Israelites to do. He didn't want them to simply plunk their tithe without putting their heart into it. He commanded them to come very purposefully and worship Him with it, saying:

When we cried to the Lord, the God of our fathers, the Lord heard our voice and looked on our affliction and our labor and our [cruel] oppression; and the Lord brought us forth out of Egypt with a mighty hand and with an outstretched arm, and with great (awesome) power and with signs and with wonders; and He brought us into this place and gave us this land, a land flowing with milk and honey. And now, behold, I bring the firstfruits of the ground which You, O Lord, have given me (verses 7-10, *The Amplified Bible*).

We would do well to say much the same thing each time we tithe. Say, "Father, once I was lost, a prisoner of sin with no hope and no covenant with You. But You sent Jesus to redeem me. You sent Him to shed His precious blood so I could be free. Thank You, Lord, for delivering me out of the kingdom of darkness and translating me into the kingdom of Your dear Son. Thank You for receiving my tithe as an expression of worship to You."

But we shouldn't stop with that. We should also say, as the Israelites did, "Now, Lord, I have brought the tithe out of my house. I haven't kept it for myself. But I've given it just as You have commanded. So look down from Your holy habitation, from heaven, and bless me!" (See verses 13-15.)

Does that kind of talk make you nervous? Do you think God will be offended if you tell Him to bless you? He won't! He'll be delighted. After all, blessing us was His idea. It's what He has wanted to do all along.

So don't be shy. Tithe boldly! Tithe gladly! Give God 10 percent of your income and 100 percent of your heart. Then rejoice in faith and say continually, "Let the Lord be magnified, Who takes pleasure in the prosperity of His servant" (Psalm 35:27, *The Amplified Bible*).

How is tithing and wealth related?

_____

_____

_____

_____

What is the connection between tithing and the heart?

_____

_____

_____

_____

When you give your tithe, what can you say to put your heart into it?

_____

_____

_____

_____

Notes:

_____

_____

_____

_____

_____

_____

_____

_____

_____

_____

_____

_____

_____

_____

_____

_____

_____

_____

_____

_____

_____

_____

_____

_____

_____

_____

_____

_____

_____

_____

_____

_____

_____

_____

_____

_____

_____

_____

Today's
Prayer of Faith

Jesus, as my Lord and High Priest, I make a commitment to bring the first fruits of my income to You and worship You with it. I rejoice in all the good which You have given to me and my household. Now, look down from heaven, and bless us as You said in Your Word. I believe I receive it, in the Name of Jesus!

Real-Life Testimonies
To Help Build Your Faith

Blessed With a Furnished Home

The Lord provided me with a home of my own and I was praying for furnishings. I was given everything I needed free of charge, including painting and decorating. Praise the Lord from whom *all* blessings flow. God bless you!

J.R.
United Kingdom

For practical tools to help you get started on a financial plan, go to kcm.org/financial-tools.

Chapter Five
Giving and the Law
of Increase

Your Heavenly Account

by Gloria Copeland

We just studied how God wants us to give our tithes—the first 10 percent of our income—with 100 percent of our hearts. After that, a major key to the prosperous life is giving *above* the tithe. God is a giver. "For God so loved the world that he *gave...*" (John 3:16).

Even if you've been struggling—if things have been tight—I have good news for you. God "is able to do exceeding abundantly above all that we ask or think, according to the power that worketh in us" (Ephesians 3:20). God desires to pour out His Glory in greater measure than ever before, not just in our hearts, lives and church services, but in our finances as well.

Now, God's abundance doesn't just fall out of heaven and hit us on the head. He has designated ways for us to receive it. If we don't know how to operate in those ways, we will miss out on what is ours.

That's really not surprising when you think about it. Even things on earth work that way. For example, you can have a million dollars in a bank account, but if you don't know it's there or if you don't know how to make a withdrawal on your account, you won't be able to enjoy that money.

The same thing is true in the kingdom of God. The Bible says you have a heavenly account. The Apostle Paul referred to it when he wrote to his partners and thanked them for giving into his ministry. "Not because I desire a gift," he said, "but I desire fruit that may abound to your account" (Philippians 4:17).

Your heavenly account is much like an earthly bank account in that you can make deposits in it. Not only is it possible to make deposits there, Jesus told us it is very important for us to do so. In Matthew 6:19-21, He said, "Lay not up for yourselves treasures upon earth, where moth and rust doth corrupt, and where thieves break through and steal: But lay up for yourselves treasures in heaven, where neither moth nor rust doth corrupt, and where thieves do not break through nor steal: for where your treasure is, there will your heart be also."

It's a wonderful thing to have an account in heaven! That's good news because the governments of this world are, for the most part, broke. They print money that doesn't have gold to back it up. They borrow money from other governments. They even borrow it from you.

But God doesn't have to print money He can't back up. His streets are gold. He owns everything. God has the greatest real estate conglomerate that ever existed. He has a lot of land leased out, but He can repossess it whenever He wants. That's what He did for the nation of Israel. He repossessed the land of Canaan, the Promised Land, from the wicked. He said to the Israelites, "Here, you can have this land. I'm giving it to you. All you have to do is go in there and take it." As Psalm 50:10 says that He owns the cattle on a thousand hills. ("And the 'taters under 'em, too!," as one fellow added.)

The Bottom Line

Once you understand you have a heavenly account into which you can make deposits, the next question you need to answer is this: How do I make those deposits?

You make them by giving to God's work.

The foundation for that giving is the tithe. When you give the first tenth of your income to the Lord, you open the door for God to come into your finances and move supernaturally. Proverbs 3:10 says that when you honor the Lord with the firstfruits of your increase "so shall your storage places be filled with plenty" *(The Amplified Bible)*.

In addition to your tithe, you also deposit into your heavenly account by giving offerings into the work of the gospel. Be sure, however, when you give, you are truly giving into a work of God. You have to put your money in good ground if you want to get a return.

If you're like me, you're already getting eager to get to the bottom line here. You're saying, "OK, I understand that I have an account. I know where it is, and I know how to make deposits. But when can I make withdrawals from this account?"

You find the answer to that question in Mark 10:29-30. Jesus was answering the disciples, who had asked Him what they were going to get in return for the giving they had done for the gospel's sake. He said, "Verily I say unto you, There is no man that hath left house, or brethren, or sisters, or father, or mother, or wife, or children, or lands, for my sake, and the gospel's, but he shall receive an hundredfold now in this time, houses, and brethren, and sisters, and mothers, and children, and lands, with persecutions; and in the world to come eternal life."

Jesus says we can receive a hundredfold return from our heavenly account today, "in this time"! Although our deposits are going to bring us an eternal reward, we don't have to wait until we die and go to heaven to draw on those resources. We can make withdrawals on our heavenly account, here and now!

Don't Let Tradition Cheat You

How do you make those withdrawals? You make them by faith. You believe in your heart and speak with your mouth that "my God supplies all my need according to His riches in glory by Christ Jesus." (See Philippians 4:19.)

You reach out with the hand of faith and claim what's yours!

A multitude of Christians are going to be surprised to find out when they get to heaven what they could have had on earth. They're going to realize, too late, that they were cheated and swindled out of their earthly inheritance by religious tradition.

They're going to find out then what you are finding out right now: God has always desired for His people to live in abundance, and all He has is ours. He put every good thing in this earth for His family. God wants you to live in a good house. He wants you to have the car you need. He wants you to be so blessed you don't even have to think about those things. He wants you to be able to think about Him instead of thinking about how you're going to buy your next tank of gas.

Listen, God isn't anywhere near broke! He has enough wealth to richly supply all of His children. Lack is not His problem. His problem has been getting His people to believe what He says in His Word about their prosperity. His problem has been getting us to be kingdom-of-God-minded in our finances.

So start now. Stop being content just to believe God for the money to make your house payment. Start believing Him for the money to pay off the entire mortgage!

God's Spirit is speaking. He's telling us it's time for us to excel in the grace of giving. As we obey, He will surely open the windows of heaven and pour out more blessings than we have room to receive.

Morning Reflection

How does giving offerings differ from the tithe?

_____

_____

_____

_____

_____

When does Jesus say we can receive a return on our giving?

_____

_____

_____

_____

How do you withdraw from your heavenly account?

_____

_____

_____

_____

Today's
Connection Points

- ### *God of Abundance* CD: "When I Believe/Give (It Shall Be Given Unto You) (Medley)" (Track 5)

  Decide to live your life to give. Let the words of this song be the cry of your heart.

- ### DVD: "Seven Things That Bring Increase" (Chapter 4)

  Listen to great teaching from Gloria on how God wants to increase you!

  Note: "Seven Things That Bring Increase" is also listed in the back of this workbook for prayerful reference.

- ### *Prosperity Scriptures* CD (Track 5)

  Genesis 39:2-4; Psalm 5:11-12; Proverbs 3:1-6, 11:27; 2 Corinthians 9:8-11

Faith
in Action

Cheerfully—and purposefully—give to the Lord.

Notes:

_____

_____

_____

_____

_____

_____

_____

_____

_____

_____

_____

_____

_____

_____

_____

_____

The Law of Increase
by Kenneth Copeland

For those who desire a life of prosperity, the verses we will look at now are absolutely crucial. They capture a law that governs everything in the kingdom of God. *Everything.* Until you begin to understand that law, you will never be able to have real spiritual success—in the area of prosperity, or anywhere else.

"Take heed what ye hear: with what measure ye mete, it shall be measured to you: and unto you that hear shall more be given. For he that hath, to him shall be given: and he that hath not, from him shall be taken even that which he hath" (Mark 4:24-25).

I call that the Law of Increase. Before you can really understand it, you first have to realize that when Jesus said the word "hear" in that passage, He wasn't simply referring to the vibrations that bounce around on your eardrums. He was talking about something much more significant.

Two people can hear the same Word. One will measure it with faith. "God has pleasure in the prosperity of His servant. Hallelujah!" he says. "I believe that with all my heart, and I'll keep on believing it until I receive that prosperity."

The other will say, "I don't care what Bible verses he comes up with, I just don't trust ol' Copeland. I'll give this prosperity stuff a try, but I doubt very much if anything will come of it. It's just too good to be true."

Both those people will receive exactly what they expect. "Be careful how you hear," Jesus said. "Because when I deal with you, I will be using your measuring stick, not Mine. However you measure it is how it will be measured back to you." One will prosper—the other won't. I can preach to you about prosperity all day long, but if you take the Word and measure it with skepticism and doubt, you still won't prosper.

(Do you want to know something funny? The skeptic will take the fact that he didn't prosper and use it to prove he was right all along! "I told you it wouldn't work and, sure enough, it didn't!")

30, 60, 100-Fold

Once you begin to understand the Law of Increase, you'll also begin to better understand what Jesus said in the Parable of the Sower in Mark 4 about the thirtyfold, sixtyfold and hundredfold return. Let's look at that in verse 20: "And these are they which are sown on good ground; such as hear the word, and receive it, and bring forth fruit, some thirtyfold, some sixty, and some an hundred."

Why is it some receive one kind of return, some another? Does God just arbitrarily give greater blessings to one person than He gives to someone else?

No! He measures the blessings back to us according to the way we measure the Word. I like the way *The Amplified Bible* puts it. It says, "Be careful what you are hearing. The measure [of thought and study] you give [to the truth you hear] will be the measure [of virtue and knowledge] that comes back to you" (verse 24).

Your prosperity depends on how much thought and study and attention you give God's Word in that area. Are you willing to give that Word first place in your heart? Are you willing to receive it in faith instead of with skepticism? Are you willing to defend it, to fight the devil when he tries to steal it? The bottom line is, just how serious are you about God's Word? Is it final authority in your life?

Taking It to Extremes

"Now Brother Copeland," you may say, "you know there are folks who have taken this message so far they've moved out of the will of God. What about them?"

It's not our business to judge them. Those people are not our servants. If you start judging them, you'll be just as far out of the will of God as they are. So just quit worrying about them.

The truth is, if Jesus showed up in the flesh, all the religious folks today would instantly brand Him as an extremist, a fanatic, just like they did in His day. He couldn't be a member in good standing of any denomination I know. So, you'd be wise not to throw labels like that around. Just leave the judging to God.

For your own protection, however, let me say this: *You become an extremist when you try to use your faith to acquire things the Word of God doesn't promise you.* That's dangerous ground.

If, for example, you announced one day that by faith you were claiming your neighbor's wife, you'd be totally off base. The Bible never promised you anybody else's wife. It says you should leave other people's spouses alone. And remember, you must have the faith to back up what you desire, and faith has to be based on the Word. You cannot receive beyond what you believe. You cannot believe beyond the Word you have stored in your heart. *"With the heart man believeth..."* (Romans 10:10).

That is the reason you need to find out what the Word says about what you desire and stand securely in faith on the promises of God.

Time in the Word

Look again at what *The Amplified Bible* says, "The measure [of thought and study] you give [to the truth you hear] will be the measure...that comes back to you..." (Mark 4:24). If you want to ensure yourself a thirtyfold, sixtyfold or even a hundredfold return, you will have to give the Word a tremendous amount of thought and study.

One of the reasons Gloria and I have seen such marvelous results in our lives and in our ministry is because when we realized what the Word of God would do, we literally immersed ourselves in it. In those early days of becoming established in God's Word, we looked around and realized that the world was coming at us from every direction. Every time we turned on the radio or the television or picked up a newspaper, we were hearing what the voices of the world had to say. So we just tuned out the world and tuned in to the Word of God instead.

It wasn't that we quit those things, we just didn't have time for them anymore. For many months we spent nearly every waking moment either reading the Word, listening to teaching on the Word or thinking about the Word.

All that time in the Word eventually had a powerful effect on us. As Romans 10:17 says, "Faith cometh by hearing, and hearing by the word of God." So we grew stronger and stronger in faith. And as that happened, we were able to increase the size of our measure!

The same thing will happen to you if you'll devote yourself to the Word. By the way, we still have to attend to God's Word if we want to continue in victory. This is a lifetime proposition.

There are a great many believers who start out devoting themselves to the Word, but they make the mistake of expecting instant, miraculous results. When that doesn't happen, they're disappointed. Don't do that.

Jesus said, "Man shall not live by bread alone, but by every word that proceedeth out of the mouth of God" (Matthew 4:4). In other words, the Word of God feeds the spirit man just as bread feeds the body. Food has to be built into your body. The vitamins and minerals it contains have a cumulative effect on it, don't they?

Much the same thing is true with the Word of God. It has a cumulative effect. Yes, at times God will act instantly and perform a miracle, but only to get things back on track. His real intention is for you to feed on His Word, to grow in strength and in faith, and to bear fruit in due season.

So don't be in such a hurry. Stay in the Word. Be patient and the results will come.

What is the Law of Increase?

_____
_____
_____
_____

What does it mean to "measure" the Word?

_____
_____
_____
_____

In what way does studying the Word have a cumulative effect?

_____
_____
_____
_____

Notes:

_____
_____
_____
_____
_____
_____
_____
_____
_____
_____
_____
_____
_____
_____
_____
_____
_____
_____
_____
_____
_____
_____

Today's

Prayer of Faith

Father, I see in Your Word that You so loved that You gave.
I set my heart to be like You and purpose to be a "cheerful,
joyous 'prompt-to-do-it' giver, whose heart is in his giving"
(2 Corinthians 9:7, The Amplified Bible).

Real-Life Testimonies
To Help Build Your Faith

Miracle Business

The first year we went to Kenneth Copeland Ministries' Southwest Believers' Convention we were living from paycheck to paycheck, wondering how we would ever get out of debt, save any money for weddings (we have three daughters and one son) or retirement. We were tithers but not givers.

Friends encouraged us to go to the Believers' Convention in Fort Worth, so we took a week's vacation to attend. We struggled to give just a couple of dollars in each of the offerings. One night we were impressed to give by faith the huge sum of $25. The next year we had increased and were able to give a little more. The third year we could hardly wait to get to Fort Worth and give. We had saved an extra $1,000 to give along with our other offerings. We were so excited to give that thousand dollars!

Four months later the most amazing thing happened! My husband was able to purchase, with a co-worker, the construction business they worked for. It was a huge, God deal!

In addition to now owning the company, he received a bonus check for $170,000—over a hundredfold return on the seed we had sown! God has continued to bless our business and increase it. Thank you for your teaching on sowing and reaping. God bless you!

Karen P.
Texas

For practical tools to help you get started on a financial plan, go to
kcm.org/financial-tools.

Chapter Six
The Secret to Receiving

Morning Connection

Looking for a Receiver
by Gloria Copeland

I'm not much of a football fan, but in January 2000, when I was watching the Super Bowl, the Lord used one particular play in that game to illustrate His goodness to me. St. Louis was playing, and at a critical point in the game, I watched as Kurt Warner drew his arm back to throw a pass. Looking down the field for someone to catch that pass, he found Isaac Bruce in position, ready and able to receive. He threw the ball. The pass was completed, and they won the Super Bowl!

Since then, I've thought about that moment again and again. God has used it to illustrate that He is always looking for a receiver, just like Kurt Warner was that day. And 1 Corinthians 2:9 tells us of the blessings God has in His hand that He is longing to pass to us—blessings beyond our comprehension: "What eye has not seen and ear has not heard and has not entered into the heart of man, [all that] God has prepared (made and keeps ready) for those who love Him [who hold Him in affectionate reverence, promptly obeying Him and gratefully recognizing the benefits He has bestowed] *(The Amplified Bible)*.

God has spiritual victories He wants us to win. He has rewards and trophies He wants us to enjoy. These wonderful things are ready when we are ready.

So what is He waiting for? He's waiting for someone to *receive!*

Of course I didn't just learn about receiving from a football game. I learned it from the Bible. Second Chronicles 16:9 says, "For the eyes of the Lord run to and fro throughout the whole earth, to show himself strong in the behalf of them whose heart is perfect toward him."

The word translated *perfect* there actually means "devoted, faithful, dedicated and consecrated." So this verse tells us that God is constantly searching for people whose hearts are devoted to Him so He can demonstrate His kindness and power in their lives. He is continually looking for a receiver.

Good Plans

No matter who you are, no matter how closely you've walked with God or how far you've run from Him, God has a plan for you. It's a good plan, too. Jeremiah 29:11 says, "'For I know the plans I have for you,' declares the Lord, 'plans to prosper you and not to harm you, plans to give you hope and a future'" *(New International Version)*.

God's plan for you is far above anything you could dream up on your own. I can vouch for that personally. Forty years ago, I could not have imagined the goodness of God that I'm enjoying now.

When I was a young girl, I wanted to be an airline stewardess. I heard they made $90 a week. That seemed like a lot of money to me and the idea of going somewhere beyond Arkansas was very exciting. Thank God, He had a higher plan for me than that. He's literally done for me what Ephesians 3:20 says: "exceeding abundantly above all that we ask or think."

Yet even so, I know that if Jesus tarries, 10 years from now His plan will take me even higher and I'll be enjoying things that right now are beyond my ability to imagine. There's no limit to the goodness of God. There's no limit to the greatness of His plan.

Once you are walking in God's will and living in His plan for your life, you'll find He also has a life of good things for you. Tradition teaches that *things* are of the devil. But the Bible teaches that God gives us richly all things to enjoy (1 Timothy 6:17). He loves for us to have wonderful things. He just doesn't want those things to have us.

Put Yourself in Position

Like a quarterback in the Super Bowl, God has His mighty arm drawn back, eager to hurl His blessings into your life. But He can't unless you are in position to receive.

So how do you put yourself in that position? Think about Isaac Bruce during the Super Bowl. Isaac wasn't distracted. He wasn't looking up in the stands to see who was watching. And he wasn't standing around with his hands in his pockets wishing he had a hamburger.

Instead Isaac was on fire to win that football game. Waiting to receive the pass, he kept his eye on the quarterback. He wasn't preoccupied with something else. He was right where he was supposed to be, intensely interested in what he was doing. He was single-minded—Isaac was ready!

So just like Isaac, in order to receive, you must be single-minded. And that means first and foremost, you seek God. You do what Matthew 6:33 says, "Seek (aim at and strive after) first of all His kingdom and His righteousness (His way of doing and being right), and then all these things taken together will be given you besides*" (The Amplified Bible). First* is the key word here! There is nothing before first. First makes everything else fall into place.

And the word *seek* in the Hebrew means "to tread frequently." Seek is a diligent word. It means "to make something your main concern, your primary pursuit." Proverbs says if you seek for God's wisdom as you seek for silver and gold, you'll find it. So when we go after God and make Him our primary pursuit, we'll begin to receive.

God has never been stingy toward His people. He has always wanted them to have the best of everything. But for us to receive the best, we have to put Him first. That's His simple formula for success.

We don't seek after things. We're not money-minded—we're God-minded. When you just go after God's blessings, you miss the Father behind those blessings...and He is the only One who makes life worth living. Money doesn't make life worth living. A good career doesn't make life worth living. The peace and joy that come from the presence of the Lord in your life—that's what makes it all worthwhile.

Morning Reflection

God has so many good things for us—what is He waiting for us to do?

_____
_____
_____
_____

What kind of plan does God have for your life?

_____
_____
_____
_____

How do you put yourself in position to receive?

_____
_____
_____
_____
_____
_____
_____

Today's Connection Points

◉ *God of Abundance* **CD: "Thank You, Lord" (Track 6)**

Receive encouragement from the Lord today as you express thanks to Him.

◉ **DVD: There is no DVD teaching today.**

◉ *Prosperity Scriptures* **CD (Track 6)**

Joshua 1:5, 7-8; 1 Samuel 2:7-10; 2 Chronicles 15:7, 17:3-6; Psalm 18:19-22; Isaiah 30:23, 48:15, 17; Ephesians 3:19-21

Faith in Action

Make a decision today to devote yourself and everything you do to the Lord.

Open your heart and your arms wide to Him so you may receive!

Notes:

_____
_____
_____
_____
_____
_____
_____
_____
_____
_____
_____
_____
_____
_____
_____
_____
_____
_____
_____
_____
_____
_____
_____
_____
_____
_____

The Secret of Receiving From God

by Kenneth Copeland

Would it be possible for someone to starve right in the middle of a supermarket?

Certainly it would. It would be absurd and unnecessary, but it could be done. A person could be wasting away from hunger, lying in the middle of the produce department floor with people offering him food left and right. But if he refused to receive it, he would eventually be as dead as can be.

I can just hear you. "That's the silliest thing I've ever heard. It would never happen!"

Naturally speaking, you're probably right. But in the realm of the spirit, things like that happen every day.

Take prosperity, for example. Second Corinthians 9:8 says, "God is able to make all grace abound toward you; that ye, always having all sufficiency in all things, may abound to every good work." Yet, how many believers do you know who are enjoying "all sufficiency in all things?" Not many, I'd guess.

If you've made Jesus the Lord of your life, you're rich. You're rich in every way—in health, in wisdom, in deliverance, in finances—because God has provided you *"all things* that pertain unto life and godliness, through the knowledge of him" (2 Peter 1:3).

But no matter how much God has made available to you, if you don't receive it, none of it will do you any good. You may have a million dollars in the bank. But if you never draw out any of it, you'll be as destitute as the poorest man in town.

Believe and Receive

The fact is, you can't receive what you don't believe! Imagine getting a letter in the mail that says you've inherited a great sum of money. If you don't believe it, how much good is that money going to do you? None at all.

That's why it's impossible to please God without faith (Hebrews 11:6). His pleasure is to prosper His servants (Psalm 35:27). And He can't get that prosperity to you if you don't have faith! You *must* believe what He says!

Hebrews 10:35-36 says, "Cast not away therefore your confidence [or faith], which hath great recompence of reward. For ye have need of patience, that, after ye have done the will of God, ye might receive the promise."

Faith and receiving are intimately connected. "Don't throw away your faith," God says, "or you won't receive the promise." Then, in verse 38, He goes on to tell you what happens if you do throw away your faith: "Now the just shall live by faith: but if any man draw back, my soul shall have no pleasure in him."

Why doesn't God have any pleasure in those who throw down their faith? Because when they throw down their faith, they throw down their connection to Him and He can't get through to them with His provision.

And let me assure you, even if you've put your faith into practice, but not yet seen results, God hasn't shortchanged you. You have everything it takes to live by faith!

The Word says, "God hath dealt to every man the measure of faith" (Romans 12:3). That means He deposited the same measure of faith inside you that He deposited in me—and in every believer on earth. It's a substance inside your spirit that's just as much a part of you as the juices in your stomach that digest your food. It's as real inside your spirit as your brain is inside your head.

Everybody's spirit has faith in it. And everybody's faith responds to the Word of God.

A Formula for Success

As a guide for you to use in receiving from your giving in any area, let me share this formula. It has worked consistently for us and will work for you if you commit yourself to it.

1. *Decide on the amount you need.* Be careful not to cheat yourself. God is a giver. Determine the amount you need and then be single-minded. A double-minded man can't receive anything from the Lord (James 1:7-8).

2. *Get in agreement according to Matthew 18:19.* This is very important. The best and most powerful situation on earth is a husband and wife who can agree together in these areas. If this isn't possible in your particular case, then get together with another believer and have him join with you.

3. *Lay hold on it by faith.* Use the principles set out in Mark 11:23-24. Believe it in your heart and confess it with your mouth.

4. *Bind the devil and his forces in the Name of Jesus.* You have the authority in Jesus' Name to order Satan out of your financial affairs. This is *your* responsibility. Don't ask God to do it. You do it in Jesus' Name. Mark 16:17, James 4:7 and Ephesians 6 tell *you* to resist the devil.

5. *Loose the forces of heaven.* Hebrews 1:14 refers to the angels as ministering spirits "sent forth to minister for them who shall be heirs of salvation." The Bible also says that angels hearken to the Word of God (Psalm 103:20), so when you speak the Word, in the Name of Jesus, they are obligated to follow your command.

6. *Praise God for the answer.* Praise keeps the door of abundance wide open. The channel between you and God is clear so you can receive from Him.

Here is an example of prayer based on these six steps:

"Father, in the Name of Jesus, we ask You for $_____. We have this money in our heavenly account and we are withdrawing this amount now. We believe we receive $_____. As in Mark 11:23-24, we believe it in our hearts and confess now that it is ours in the Name of Jesus. We agree that we have $_____ according to Matthew 18:19. From this day forward, we roll the care of this over on You and thank You for it.

"Satan, in the Name of Jesus, we take authority over you; we bind your operation now and render you helpless.

"Ministering spirits, we charge you to go forth and cause this amount to come to us according to Hebrews 1:14.

"Father, we praise Your Name for meeting our needs according to Your riches in glory by Christ Jesus and for multiplying our seed for sowing. In the Name of Jesus. Amen."

Now, get ready to receive…because your victory is closer than you can imagine!

Evening Reflection

How is believing connected with receiving?

_____
_____
_____
_____

How can you be confident that you have faith?

_____
_____
_____
_____
_____
_____
_____
_____

Write a prayer for your own situation based on the Formula for Success:

_____

_____

_____

_____

Notes:

_____

_____

_____

_____

_____

_____

_____

_____

_____

_____

_____

_____

_____

_____

_____

_____

_____

_____

_____

_____

_____

_____

_____

_____

_____

_____

_____

_____

_____

_____

_____

_____

_____

_____

_____

_____

_____

_____

_____

Today's
Prayer of Faith

Father, according to Your Word, I stand in unshakable faith, based on Your Word, ready to receive from You. I am a tither and a giver. Thank You for providing exceeding abundantly above all that I could ask or think. Thank You that You meet all my needs according to Your riches in glory by Christ Jesus and for multiplying my seed sown so that I may give into every good work. In Jesus' Name. Amen!

Real-Life Testimonies
To Help Build Your Faith

Completely Debt Free

I have known for some time the Lord wanted me debt free, and my only debt was a mortgage. On a piece of paper, I wrote the amount I needed and placed it on my refrigerator. Every time I saw it, I thanked Him that I was debt free. I arrived at work January 3 to see an envelope on my desk addressed to me from my boss of 30 years. He gave me a $100,000 bonus! I am so grateful to the Lord for answered prayer, and grateful my boss was the channel through whom I received this blessing.

E.C.
Texas

For practical tools to help you get started on a financial plan, go to kcm.org/financial-tools.

Chapter Seven
A Prosperous Soul

Build Your Financial Foundation
by Gloria Copeland

Never try to build a house without first laying a foundation.

I don't care how eager you are to get it finished, how excited you are about filling it with furniture and decorating it all just right—take the time to put down a solid foundation first. If you don't, that house will be so unstable it will soon come tumbling down.

That's simple advice, isn't it? Everyone with any sense at all knows it. Yet in the spiritual realm, people make that mistake all the time. They see a blessing God has promised them in His Word, and they are so eager to have it, they ignore the foundational basics of godly living and pursue just that one thing.

That's especially true in the area of prosperity. Often, people are so desperate for a quick financial fix, they just pull a few prosperity promises out of the Bible and try to believe them—without allowing God to change anything else in their lives. Of course, it doesn't work, and those people end up disappointed. Sometimes they even come to the conclusion that it wasn't God's will for them to prosper after all.

But we know from the Word of God that it is definitely God's will for all of His children to prosper! We saw that in the very first session of this LifeLine study. The Apostle John wrote, "Beloved, I wish above all things that thou mayest prosper and be in health, even as thy soul prospereth" (3 John 2). Notice that John didn't just say, "I want you to prosper." He said, "I want you to prosper as your soul prospers." He tied prosperity in all areas of our lives to the prosperity of our minds, wills and emotions.

God's plan is for us to grow financially as we grow spiritually. He knows it is dangerous to put great wealth into the hands of someone who is too spiritually immature to handle it. You can see dramatic evidence of that fact in the lives of people who have acquired financial riches through this world's system, apart from God. In most cases, such riches just help people to die younger and in more misery than they would have if they'd been poorer.

That's because they use their wealth to sin in greater measure. They use it to pay for an immoral lifestyle that eventually destroys them. The wages of sin is death. That is an inescapable fact. So, when people get money and use it to sin, it does them more harm than good. As Proverbs 1:32 says, "...the prosperity of fools shall destroy them."

Seek First Things First

In light of that truth, it's easy to see why God wants us to increase financially at the same rate we increase spiritually. He wants us to outgrow our fleshly foolishness so our prosperity will bring us blessing and not harm.

"But Gloria," you say, "I need financial help fast!"

Then get busy growing. Get busy building your foundation for prosperity.

How? By finding out what God says in His Word and doing it.

You see, the foundation for prosperity is a continual lifestyle built on the Word of God. It is doing whatever God tells you to do, thinking whatever He tells you to think, and saying whatever He tells you to say.

Godly prosperity is the result of putting God's Word—all of it, not just the parts about financial prosperity—first place in your life. It comes when you apply His principles on a continual basis—not just because you want money, but because Jesus is your Lord and you want to follow Him. It comes when you start obeying the instructions He gave us in Matthew 6:33: "Seek (aim at and strive after) first of all His kingdom and His righteousness (His way of doing and being right), and then all these things taken together will be given you besides" *(The Amplified Bible).*

I remember back before Ken and I knew we could trust God to take care of us financially, I thought it was my job to worry about how we were going to pay our bills. I spent a great deal of my time thinking things like, *What am I going to do about this light bill? How am I going to keep the electricity from being shut off?* To me it would have been irresponsible not to worry about such things!

Then I found out it wasn't God's will for me to worry (Matthew 6:25-33). It was His will for us to believe Him to care for us. I also learned that as believers, we're not to seek after material riches. We're not to pursue money like people do who are without God. They have to pursue it. They don't have a covenant with God, so if they don't seek material goods, they won't get them!

But we're not like those people. We're not in the world without God and without a covenant (Ephesians 2:12-13). We have God's promise of provision. He has assured us in His Word that He will not only meet our needs, but give us abundance.

It's important for us to remember, however, that a covenant is always between two parties. It has two sides to it. A covenant says, *If you do this, then I'll do that.*

God's part of the covenant is to prosper us—spirit, soul and body as well as financially. What is our part of the covenant? It's not to seek after that prosperity. If we do that, we'll get sidetracked. Our part of the covenant is to seek first His kingdom, His way of doing and being right!

Our part is to say, "Lord, I'll do whatever You tell me to do. I'll obey Your Word and do what is right in Your sight—even if it looks like it will cost me."

Of course, obeying God's Word never costs in the long run. It pays! You always put yourself in a position for increase when you seek after God and do things His way.

Build the Whole House

With that foundation laid, you'll be ready to step out in faith and receive the abundance God has in store for you.

Many people who have lived godly lives have failed to do that so they've missed out on God's financial blessings. Although they've continually applied the principles of God's Word and become prime candidates for great prosperity, they've unwittingly passed it by because religious tradition has taught them that God wants them in poverty. Christians like that have great wealth in their spiritual bank account, but because they don't realize it's there, they never tap in to it!

Don't let that happen to you. Don't just build the foundation for prosperity and stop there. Go on and build the whole house. Dare to believe that if you'll seek first God's kingdom, His way of doing and being right, all other things (the food, the clothes, the cars, the houses, everything!) will be added to you as well.

Build your foundation, then dare to believe—and you will surely prosper!

Morning Reflection

What is the foundation for a prosperous life?

_____

_____

_____

_____

_____

_____

Why is it important to lay a foundation for a prosperous life?

_____

_____

_____

_____

What is God's part and our part in building a prosperous life?

_____

_____

_____

_____

Today's Connection Points

- *God of Abundance* **CD: There is no music track for today.**
- **DVD: "Seek and Receive" (Chapter 5)**

  Gloria teaches when you seek God first, you'll receive all you need...and more!

- *Prosperity Scriptures* **CD (Track 7)**

  Deuteronomy 2:7, 8:7-10, 32:13; 2 Chronicles 29:2, 32:27-29; Psalm 34:10; Philippians 4:19; Ephesians 3:20

Faith in Action

Make a decision to seek God first today.
Read His Word, think His thoughts, walk in His truth!

Notes:

_____

_____

_____

_____

_____

_____

_____

_____

_____

_____

_____

_____

_____

_____

_____

_____

_____

Prosper From the Inside Out
by Kenneth Copeland

Whether they admit it or not, a great many believers have trouble believing—really believing—they'll ever be financially prosperous. You can show them what the Word of God says. You can load them up with scriptures that prove God's will for them is prosperity…and they'll agree with every word. But they'll still go home and live poor. When they look at their mountain of bills, the faltering economy and their dead-end jobs, they just can't see how God could possibly prosper them. *After all, what's He going to do?* they wonder. *Start floating twenty dollar bills down from the trees?*

How *does* God prosper His people? We find that answer in 3 John 2, written by John through the inspiration of the Holy Ghost: "Beloved, I wish above all things that thou mayest prosper and be in health, even as thy soul prospereth."

I want you to notice something. That scripture doesn't say I pray you prosper even as the economy prospers or even as your employer decides to promote you. It says I pray you prosper as your *soul* prospers.

That's where most believers miss it when it comes to receiving financial prosperity. They keep looking at situations outside themselves, thinking that's where their hope lies. But God doesn't work from the outside in. He works from the inside out.

He blesses you materially as your soul prospers on His Word. Then, as the seeds of prosperity are planted in your mind, your will and your emotions, and as you allow those seeds to grow, they eventually produce a great financial harvest—no matter how bad the conditions around you may be.

Read the story of Joseph in Genesis 37-41 and you can see exactly what I'm talking about. When Joseph was sold as a slave to the Egyptians, he didn't have a dime to his name. He didn't even have his freedom. But, right in the middle of his slavery, God gave Joseph such wisdom and ability that he made his owner, Potiphar, rich. As a result, Potiphar put Joseph in charge of all his possessions.

Later, Potiphar's wife got mad at Joseph, and he ended up in prison. Talk about a dead-end job! There's really not much chance for advancement in prison, is there? But God gave him insight that no other man in Egypt had. He gave him such great wisdom that he ended up on Pharaoh's staff—not as a slave but as the most honored man in the entire country next to Pharaoh, himself. From prison to prime minister.

He rode along in a chariot and people literally bowed down before him. During a world-wide famine, Joseph was in charge of *all* the food. Now that's prosperity!

How did God accomplish that? By prospering Joseph's soul. No matter how dismal Joseph's situation became, no matter how impossible his problems, God was able to reveal the spiritual secrets that would open the door of success for him.

That's what makes God's method of prospering so exciting. It works anywhere and everywhere. It will work in the poorest countries on the face of this earth just like it will work here in the United States. I've seen it happen.

The Spirit of Truth

God doesn't want you groping around in the dark. He wants to reveal His secrets to you, secrets that will prosper you and make you successful in every area of your life—including your finances.

That's why He's given you the Holy Spirit. Do you have any idea what a tremendous resource He is? Most believers don't. They get in church and say, "Oh, yes, amen, brother. Thank God for the Holy Spirit. Praise God. Hallelujah." Then they go home and forget about Him.

It's not that they aren't sincere on Sunday. They are. They genuinely appreciate the little bit they understand about the Holy Spirit. But they haven't learned how to tap in to the unlimited wisdom and power He can make available to them in their daily lives.

Jesus said, "Howbeit when he, the Spirit of truth, is come, he will guide you into all truth: for he shall not speak of himself; but whatsoever he shall hear, that shall he speak: and he will show you things to come" (John 16:13).

Read that verse again and think about it.

Jesus said the Holy Spirit would guide us into *all* truth! Not just enough truth to get by on. Not just an occasional truth to help us teach our Sunday school classes. *All* truth!

If you're a businessman, that means the Holy Spirit will show you how to increase your profits and reduce your expenses. If you're a mother, it means the Holy Spirit will show you how to settle arguments between your children. If you're a student, it means the Holy Spirit will show you how to excel in your classes.

In fact, if you know Jesus Christ as your Lord and are baptized in the Holy Spirit, somehow inside you is the answer to every financial problem, every spiritual problem, and every physical problem that exists. You have answers for problems you don't even know about yet.

There are so many people standing around wringing their hands and worrying. "God could never prosper me," they say. "All I get is this little paycheck...and my company's losing money, so I know they're not going to give me a raise. How on earth is God going to prosper me?"

Maybe He'll give you an idea that will turn your company's loss into a profit. Maybe He'll give you an idea for a new product and you'll start your own company.

God has probably already given you idea after idea that would have made you rich if you'd just had spiritual sense enough to recognize them. But, you didn't even know they were there because you weren't paying attention to the things of God. You weren't seeking revelation of the "secret things." You were probably too busy watching TV and listening to some announcer tell you which brand of toothpaste to buy or how bad the economy is.

Listen to me: The Holy Spirit isn't going to be able to get through to you while you're lying around watching television. He's a gentleman. He just isn't going to come, grab the remote control out of your hand, and shout, "Hey! I have some important things to tell you!"

No. He'll wait quietly for you to shut off all that other junk that's been occupying your mind and tune in to Him.

Right here is where most believers miss it. They're so involved in life, and even so involved in church activities and religious organizations that they don't ever have any time to spend with the Lord. They never just stop and fellowship with Him. All He gets is a few moments with them as they drive down the freeway or a few minutes between television commercials...and most of that is filled with "poor ol' me."

There are believers God has wanted to put into high political offices. He would have shown them how to solve some of this nation's problems, but He couldn't get their attention. So He just left them where they were, spinning their wheels in a dead-end job. There are others God would have promoted until they became chief executives of major corporations, but they were too busy working toward their own little goals to find out what His goals were.

Don't miss out on God's plans of prosperity for you. Spend time with Him. Listen to Him and learn to recognize His voice.

Get Serious

Now, it's going to take more than a couple of Bible verses and a five-minute prayer to tap in to the revelations the Holy Spirit has for you. You'll have to get serious about it.

If you think you don't have time to do that, think again.

How many hours a day do you spend in front of the television? How many hours a week do you spend reading the newspaper? How many hours reading novels and looking at magazines? How much time thinking about your problems?

Replace those things with the Word of God. Use that time to meditate on the Sriptures. Get in prayer and say, "Holy Spirit, I need to know what to do regarding this situation I'm in." Then listen. He'll start giving you the wisdom of God concerning your finances (or any other part of your life).

Will He really? Sure He will. James 1:5-6 says: "If any of you lack wisdom, let him ask of God, that giveth to all men liberally, and upbraideth not; and it shall be given him. But let him ask in faith, nothing wavering. For he that wavereth is like a wave of the sea driven with the wind and tossed."

Again, though, let me warn you: We're talking about digging into the Word and staying there until you begin to hear from the Holy Spirit and until you develop a faith that doesn't waver. That's not something that happens overnight. Like a spiritual farmer, you must plant and weed and water the Word within you. It will take some time and some work, but believe me, the harvest will be well worth the effort.

Evening Reflection

How does God prosper His people?

_____
_____
_____
_____

What part does the Holy Spirit play in making you prosperous?

_____
_____
_____
_____

How do you "get serious" about the revelations the Holy Spirit has for you?

_____
_____
_____
_____

Notes:

_____
_____
_____
_____
_____
_____
_____
_____
_____
_____
_____
_____
_____
_____
_____
_____
_____
_____
_____

Today's
Prayer of Faith

Holy Spirit, I make myself available to You. Open the Word to me and show me revelation that will change my life forever. I determine to seek God with all my heart. Help me, day by day, to develop a faith that will not waver! In Jesus' Name. Amen.

Real-Life Testimonies
To Help Build Your Faith

Repentance Unlocks God's Provision

In October, I received an eviction notice and owed $1600 in back rent. I was laid off in June and had also been in the hospital, ill. God provided the $1600 back rent and alleviated all financial pressure. I received a new, low-mileage car, paid in full; a cell phone for two years; perfume I wanted; and I was healed of high blood pressure—no more medication! Your instructions on repentance and overflow were key. Thank you for your help and love as a covenant Partner.

P.H.
Oklahoma

For practical tools to help you get started on a financial plan, go to kcm.org/financial-tools.

Chapter Eight
God Can Turn Your Situation Around

The Unbeatable Spirit of Faith
by Gloria Copeland

No matter how difficult a situation you may be facing today, God can turn it around!

Your bank account may be empty and the creditors knocking on the door. The doctors may have told you there's no hope. There may be trouble in your family or on your job. Your problems may be stacked so high, you feel like you can never overcome them. But don't let the devil fool you. He has never devised a problem that faith in God can't fix.

Nothing intimidates God. It's as easy for Him to buy you a new home as it is for Him to pay your rent. It's just as easy for God to heal cancer as it is for Him to heal a headache.

Even in times like these, when the whole world seems to be in trouble, God can bring you through in triumph. He can do for you what He did for the Israelites. Exodus 10 says when darkness covered the nation of Egypt where they lived—a darkness so thick the Egyptians couldn't see each other or move for three days—"all the children of Israel had light in their dwellings" (verse 23).

Think about that! If you'll dare to believe God's Word, you can have light in the middle of a dark world. You can live prosperously in the middle of an impoverished world. You can have protection in the middle of a dangerous world. You can live healed in the middle of a sick world. You can live free in the middle of a captive world.

But let me warn you, you can't do it by dragging around in an attitude of defeat. If you want to walk in constant victory, you must develop a spirit of faith and persevere in that spirit even when the devil is putting pressure on you.

People with the spirit of faith always receive the blessings of God. They may go through tests and trials but they come out supernaturally every time.

I like those odds, don't you? I like to beat the devil every time. And, glory to God, we can do it if we'll walk continually in the spirit of faith.

The Apostle Paul gives us some powerful insight about how to cultivate that spirit in 2 Corinthians 4. Read carefully what he says: "We having the same spirit of faith, according as it is written, I believed, and therefore have I spoken; we also believe, and therefore speak.... While we look not at the things which are seen, but at the things which are not seen: for the things which are seen are temporal; but the things which are not seen are eternal" (verses 13, 18).

Open the Window

The first and most fundamental fact these verses reveal about the spirit of faith is that it *believes.*

What does it believe? The Word of God. What's more, faith believes God's Word just because God said it—whether natural circumstances seem to agree or not.

That means if you want to maintain a spirit of faith in the area of finances, for example, you must start by getting your Bible and finding out what God has said about prosperity. Then you must choose to receive that Word as the truth. Don't shut your heart to it by saying, "Well, that's not the way my church teaches it," or "That's not what my grandmother taught me." Just say, "The Word says prosperity belongs to me and I believe it!"

Then keep putting the Word in your heart day after day until faith rises up within you and your finances begin to line up with that Word.

Why is it so important for you to develop your faith? Because faith is what connects you to the blessings of God. It's the force that gives those blessings substance in your life (Hebrews 11:1). And besides all that, it pleases God (verse 6).

It's faith that reaches into the realm of the spirit, grasps the promise of God and brings forth a tangible, physical fulfillment of that promise. It brings spiritual blessings. It brings the car you need, or the healing for your body. It brings action in this earth.

Romans 5:2 says we have access by faith into the grace of God. Therefore, if you want grace for the new birth, you must receive it by faith. If you want God's grace for healing, you must receive it by faith. If you want God's grace in your finances or any other area of your life, you must get it by faith.

I like to think of it this way: When you believe the Word of God, you open the window of your life to give God the opportunity to move there.

Oddly enough, that bothers some people. They can't understand why God needs *an opportunity.* After all, He is God. Can't He do anything He wants?

Yes, He can. And He wants to respond to our faith.

You see, He is not like the devil. He doesn't force Himself on you. He waits for you to give Him an opening by believing His Word.

We Believe...Therefore We Speak

That's what Abraham did. When God told him that he and Sarah were going to have a baby, Abraham just took God at His Word. In light of the circumstances, that was quite a step of faith. After all, Abraham was 100 years old and Sarah was 90 and barren.

Most people would have been overwhelmed by those problems. But not Abraham. He "believed God, and it was counted unto him for righteousness" (Romans 4:3). Even though, in the natural realm, it was impossible for what God said to come to pass, Abraham believed God anyway.

That's what the spirit of faith does. It stands in the midst of the most impossible circumstances and believes God anyway! Then it begins to speak.

It doesn't say just any old thing, either. It speaks the Word of God. When the bills stack up, faith doesn't say, "I'm drowning in debt." Faith says, "My God supplies all my needs according to His riches in glory by Christ Jesus. He is able to do exceeding abundantly above all I can ask or think!"

"Well, I'm just not comfortable with that confession business. I like to believe God quietly."

That may be what you like, but it's not what the Bible teaches. The Bible says, *we believe, therefore we speak* (2 Corinthians 4:13). If you want to change your circumstances, you must have faith in two places—in your heart and in your mouth.

That's why God changed Abram's name to Abraham. *Abraham* means "father of many nations." So every time Abraham introduced himself after his name was changed, he was actually saying, "Hello. How are you? I'm the father of many nations." To most people that probably sounded ridiculous because, at the time, Abraham was still a childless old man married to a barren old woman. I'm sure they thought Abraham was a little crazy.

But he wasn't. He was simply following the example of God, Himself, "who quickeneth the dead, and calleth those things which be not as though they were" (Romans 4:17). By speaking in faith, Abraham was doing exactly what God did when He created the earth.

Read Genesis 1 and you'll see what I mean. There the Bible tells us that in the beginning "the earth was without form, and void; and darkness was upon the face of the deep" (verse 2). Yet God didn't look at that darkness and say, "Oh my, the earth sure is a dark place!" If He had, the earth would have *remained* a dark place.

No, God changed the natural circumstance by calling things that be not as though they were. He looked at the darkness and said, "Light be!" and light was. God spoke out by faith what He wanted to come to pass. That's how we operate too, when we're living by the spirit of faith.

One thing you must understand. I'm not just talking about saying God's Word once or twice. I'm talking about consistently speaking words of faith. If you get on your knees in prayer and say, "I believe I receive my financial needs met, in Jesus' Name," then go to dinner with your friends and say, "I'm going bankrupt. I can't find a job. I'm about to lose my home. I don't know what I'm going to do," you won't get anywhere.

It's what you say *continually* that comes to pass in your life. So, if you're believing God for finances, make it a habit to say things like this: "According to Deuteronomy 28, lack is a curse of the law. And Galatians 3:13 says Jesus has redeemed me from that curse. Therefore I'm redeemed from the curse of lack!"

Then every time your bills come to mind, call them paid in the Name of Jesus. Call yourself prosperous. Call yourself debt free. Be like Abraham and by the spirit of faith call things that be not as though they were.

Keep Your Eyes on the Word

Right now you may be thinking, *I really want to do that. I want to walk and talk by faith. The problem is, every time I look at the mess I'm in, I get discouraged.*

Then stop looking at that mess! Instead, focus your attention on the promise of God. Keep His Word in front of your eyes and in your ears until you can *see* it coming to pass with the eyes of your spirit.

That's what the spirit of faith does. It looks "not at the things which are seen, but at the things which are not seen: for the things which

are seen are temporal; but the things which are not seen are eternal" (2 Corinthians 4:18).

Of course, I'm not saying you should ignore your problems or close your eyes to them as if they aren't real. They are real. But according to the Word they are *temporal*. That means "subject to change." And you can be assured that if you keep looking at the Word, they *will* change!

Morning
Reflection

What does it mean to have a spirit of faith?

_____

_____

_____

_____

What does the spirit of faith say?

_____

_____

_____

_____

What should be your response to discouragement?

_____

_____

_____

_____

Today's
Connection Points

⊙ *God of Abundance* CD: "More Than Enough" (Track 7)

As you put your faith and finances in order, rejoice that Jesus, Himself, is more than enough!

⊙ DVD: "Words of Faith" (Chapter 6)

Kenneth teaches how your words can make or break your success.

⊙ *Prosperity Scriptures* CD (Track 8)

Genesis 12:1-3, 26:1-3; Deuteronomy 6:18, 28:13; Nehemiah 9:21; Psalm 36:7-10, 37:11, 103:2-5, 107:31-32, 35-38; Proverbs 10:22, 13:22; Luke 4:18; 2 Corinthians 8:9; Galatians 3:13-14, 29; Ephesians 1:17-23; 1 Timothy 6:17-19; 1 Peter 3:9-12

Faith in Action

Don't give up!
Stand in faith, knowing that God desires a full, debt-free and prosperous life for you!

Notes:

_____
_____
_____
_____
_____
_____
_____
_____
_____
_____
_____
_____
_____
_____
_____
_____
_____
_____
_____
_____
_____
_____
_____
_____
_____
_____
_____
_____
_____
_____
_____
_____
_____
_____
_____
_____
_____
_____
_____
_____

Getting Out of Debt
by Kenneth Copeland

When I first started hearing what the Word had to say about finances, I was $22,000 in debt. I don't mean I was just behind on current bills. Those debts were all outstanding. Most of my creditors never expected a dime from me. It looked like there was no hope at all.

Right in the middle of that situation, Gloria and I caught hold of the Word. We saw that there was power in the Word. We saw that deliverance was in the Word. And somehow God helped us understand that the more we fed our spirits the Word, the stronger our faith would grow and God could turn our situation around.

So, we made a decision. We set our hearts to be obedient to the Word. We agreed that we would take every truth we saw there and apply it in our lives—whether we felt like it or not.

Not long after that, we ran into a scripture that said, "Owe no man any thing, but to love one another..." (Romans 13:8). That hit me hard. I said, "Oh God, surely You're not telling me not to ever borrow money. Please, don't tell me that! You're already speaking to me about a world-wide ministry, and now You're coming around telling me not to borrow any money? Those two just don't mix!"

I even ran and got *The Amplified Bible* in hopes that it would translate that verse differently. You know what it said? *"Keep out of debt...."* That left me in worse trouble than ever.

Believe me, at first I had a tough time measuring that scripture to my advantage. *I've had it either way I go,* I thought. *I'm hung if I do and I'm hung if I don't. If I don't borrow the money, I'll never be able to do what God has instructed me to do in worldwide ministry. If I do borrow the money, I'll be out of His will. What will I do?*

I was in a real quandary about it for a while. Then Gloria and I talked about it and we came to an agreement. "We can't turn back now," we said. "We've made a quality decision, and we won't retreat from it. We'll stick with the Word of God no matter what. We'll believe that somehow it will turn out to our advantage."

I didn't know enough back then to understand how it could turn out to our advantage. I just knew enough about the nature of God and the nature of His Word to know that it would. Quite honestly, I didn't choose to obey that scripture because I thought it would make me prosperous. If I had been looking for wealth, I would have looked somewhere else. I put that scripture into action in my life strictly because that's what God told me to do.

But I wasn't the only one having a real struggle. It was difficult for Gloria to measure it to her advantage, too. We were living in a terrible little house at the time. (Just to give you an idea of how bad it was, they eventually tore down the whole block right up to our house.) She wanted a new home more than just about any, natural thing.

How could we ever buy a decent house without borrowing? It didn't seem possible. So, to her, it was as if that scripture had said, "Gloria, you can't have a new house."

But she refused to measure it that way. She grabbed the devil by the throat and said, "Look here now, you're not cheating me out of my house." Then she started believing that somehow God could provide her with a debt-free house, even though in her own mind she couldn't understand how that could happen.

Now, after more than 25 years, we can look back and see that trusting God instead of borrowing has been the greatest financial decision we've ever made. We can see how God paid off that $22,000 debt I owed, how He financed the ministry, how He provided the home of our choice, how He met every need and fulfilled every desire of our hearts. Now, it's easier to read, "Owe no man any thing, but to love one another," and measure it with faith and joy.

Keeping Out of Debt

Unless I miss my guess, right now your mind is going off in every direction. *Is he saying it's a sin to borrow money? Oh, my goodness, I'll never get by without borrowing money! My church even borrows money—surely, my church can't be wrong!, etc., etc.*

First of all, let me assure you, I didn't say it was a sin for you to borrow money. I didn't say it was not a sin either. That's for you and God to determine. As you seek His will on the matter, however, be sure to seriously consider what He's already said about the subject in His Word. For example:

- "Keep out of debt and owe no man anything, except to love one another" (Romans 13:8, *The Amplified Bible*).
- "When the Lord your God blesses you as He promised you, then you shall lend to many nations, but you shall not borrow; and you shall rule over many nations, but they shall not rule over you" (Deuteronomy 15:6, *The Amplified Bible*).
- "The Lord shall open unto thee his good treasure, the heaven to give the rain unto thy land in his season, and to bless all the work of thine hand: and thou shalt lend unto many nations, and thou shalt not borrow. And the Lord shall make thee the head, and not the tail; and thou shalt be above only, and thou shalt not be beneath; if that thou hearken unto the commandments of the Lord thy God, which I command thee this day, to observe and to do them" (Deuteronomy 28:12-13).
- "The borrower is servant to the lender" (Proverbs 22:7).

It seems to me, those scriptures speak for themselves. It is your decision whether you want to be the head and not the tail. Furthermore, when you borrow and go into debt to someone else, you look to him as your source of supply. Wouldn't you rather have God as your source?

You may be thinking, *Well, what can I do? I'm already up to my neck in debt.*

If you want to be free, just make a commitment before God to get out from under those debts. It won't happen overnight, but it will happen if you'll obey God and stay on the Word.

Remember that $22,000 worth of bad debt I told you about? At the time I committed to God to pay that off and never borrow another dime, it looked to me like I'd never be able to do it. But in faith I sat down and wrote out checks in payment of each debt. Then I put them in a drawer and waited for God to provide the money. As He did, I'd go to the drawer, get out the check and pay off a debt. Within 11 months, I was free and clear of debt. During that time, we began an increase that has never stopped. It is THE BLESSING of God.

"Oh, Brother Copeland, do you think God would enable me to pay off my debts that fast?"

I don't know. How serious are you about the Word? How much time and attention are you willing to give it? How obedient are you willing to be?

God didn't make it possible for me to pay off my debts just because He liked me a little more than most folks. No, He's no respecter of persons, but He *is* a respecter of faith. He's a respecter of obedience. So, it's really up to you, isn't it? However you choose to measure it, is how He'll measure it back to you.

As you look at your situation right now, you may not be able to see how on earth you could ever get out of debt, much less stay that way. Don't worry, I felt that way, too, at first. I just didn't see how I'd ever be able to operate successfully without borrowing money. The bottom line is, you have to trust God!

He knows how, and He showed me. He'll do the same for you.

Evening Reflection

What does Scripture say concerning debt?

_____
_____
_____
_____

What does Proverbs 22:7 mean when it says the "borrower is servant to the lender"?

_____
_____
_____
_____

What is your first step to complete debt freedom?

_____
_____
_____
_____

Notes:

_____
_____
_____
_____
_____
_____
_____
_____
_____
_____
_____
_____
_____
_____
_____
_____
_____
_____
_____
_____
_____
_____

Today's Prayer of Faith

Father, I believe and say that I am prosperous in the Name of Jesus. My debts are paid in full and I have more than I can contain. You have made me the head and not the tail, above only and not beneath. I know by Your Word that it is Your will that I be debt free and owe no man anything but to love him. So, through the eye of faith, I see myself debt free. I will speak Your Word, only, concerning my debt freedom and prosperity! In Jesus' Name. Amen.

Real-Life Testimonies
To Help Build Your Faith

Refuse to Quit...and Win!

In 1996 my husband, Steve, had a word from the Lord telling him we would have a warm house, be out of debt and have $50,000 in the bank. We stood on that promise and never doubted it would come to pass, even though we were $119,000 in debt at the time.

On July 2, 2001, we confidently sowed a seed at the West Coast Believers' Convention for the sale of our campground, fully expecting that when we returned home from the convention, it would be sold. When it still hadn't sold in 2003, Steve got mad at the devil and taped the canceled check to our computer monitor. Every time the devil said, "The campground won't sell," we laid hands on the check and believed it was sold. We never gave up or dug up our seed, and finally our campground sold in March 2005.

Today we are completely debt free. We have a house that is warm in winter, cool in summer and totally paid for. We also have more than $50,000 in the bank, and a new car paid in full! God is faithful to keep His promise, if we don't quit!

Beryl H.
Montana

For practical tools to help you get started on a financial plan, go to kcm.org/financial-tools.

Chapter Nine
The Economy, the Enemy and the Believer

Defeating Satan's Attacks

by Gloria Copeland

When you begin to prosper, or even just stand for your prosperity, you may find yourself in for more than you bargained for. Satan will do what he can to get you to give up and go back right where you've been all your life. But don't do it! Instead, prepare yourself and defeat his attack with the Word.

Make a Decision

The first step in defeating Satan's attack against you is to make the decision that you are not going to allow him to change your confession of faith that you believe you received when you prayed. The decision of your will—to stand and continue to stand, regardless of Satan's tactics and pressure—will enable you to accomplish the will of God and receive and carry away what is promised. Your decision will cause the power of patience to undergird your faith. Patience is the quality that does not surrender to circumstances.

Do not be willing to entertain any imagination or high thing that Satan exalts against the knowledge of God's Word. If God's Word says you have the answer, don't let Satan take it from you.

Resist the Devil

The second step in stopping Satan's attack to defeat your faith is to resist the devil. "Submit yourselves therefore to God. Resist the devil, and he will flee from you" (James 4:7). You have submitted yourself to the obedience of God's Word. Therefore, refuse to receive or give thought to anything that exalts itself against God's Word.

Do what my daughter did to me when she was about 3 years old. I said, "Kellie, pick up your toys." She answered, as she walked away, "That's not my thought." That's the way you have to do Satan. If he hits you with doubt, defeat or discouragement, tell him, "That's not my thought!"

Don't give your thought life to Satan's temptation. Don't dwell on his threats, just rebuke them. *Worry* is meditating on the words of the devil. Don't tolerate that. Meditate on God's Word. Resist the devil and resist him quickly. Don't allow him to hang around, pressuring your mind. At the first symptom of lack, command Satan to flee. Do not procrastinate.

Give Your Attention to God's Word

The third step in defeating Satan's attack is to give your attention to God's Word. Proverbs 4:20-23 says, "My son, attend to my words; incline thine ear unto my sayings. Let them not depart from thine eyes; keep them in the midst of thine heart. For they are life unto those that find them, and health to all their flesh. Keep thy heart with all diligence; for out of it are the issues of life." The more attention you give God's Word, the easier the other steps will be in resisting Satan's attacks.

Keep God's Word in front of your eyes and in the midst of your heart. Satan tries to divert your attention from the Word to circumstances. God's Word says that abundance belongs to you. Satan says, "It does not. Look and see." That's how Satan sells his bad news to you: through your senses—what you can see, hear and feel.

Refuse to be moved by what you see—be moved only by what God's Word says.

Refuse to be moved by what you hear—be moved only by what God's Word says.

Refuse to be moved by what you feel—be moved only by what God's Word says.

Refuse to be moved by circumstances—be moved only by what God's Word says.

Yes, your senses can be trained on the Word of God. They are trained by practice—the practice of continually demanding them to act on God's Word.

Refuse to Speak Contrary

The fourth step in overcoming Satan's temptations is to refuse to speak words contrary to what you believe you have received.

Continually speak the Word of God in the face of adversity. Satan is after your words so he can use them against you. Refuse to let him influence your words. Speak words of faith. You will have what you say. Make your words agree with what you desire to come to pass. Learn to answer every doubt or fear immediately with the Word of God.

Count It All Joy!

"My brethren, count it all joy when ye fall into divers [various] temptations; knowing this, that the trying of your faith worketh patience. But let patience have her perfect work, that ye may be perfect and entire, wanting nothing" (James 1:2-4).

Finally, count it all joy. Why? *Because this is one more opportunity for you to prove that the Word of God works.* You have a covenant with God. You have authority over Satan. You have the Name of Jesus and the gifts of the Spirit. This test and trial will be like the others in which God's Word brought you victory.

Count it all joy because you know that the trying of your faith works (exercises) patience. You will not be moved off the Word of God.

Your patience will not yield to circumstances or succumb to trial.

"Blessed is the man that endureth temptation: for when he is tried, he shall receive the crown of life, which the Lord hath promised to them that love him" (James 1:12). When the Bible says *blessed,* it means *blessed!* Every man is not blessed. The blessed man is one who endures temptation without yielding to Satan's pressure to faint and give up what belongs to him in God's Word. The man is blessed who trusts in his covenant with God to provide whatever he needs.

When he is tried, he shall receive. This man has been tried and found faithful to God's Word. Satan, himself, has proven the man's faith. There is nothing left for that man but to receive what he has asked of God. He receives whatever he has trusted God's Word to obtain. God will establish His covenant in his life!

Morning Reflection

What are the five steps to defeating Satan's attacks?

1. _____
2. _____
3. _____
4. _____
5. _____

How does the enemy use your senses to discourage you?

_____
_____
_____
_____

Why should you "count it all joy" when you are tempted?

_____
_____
_____
_____
_____
_____
_____

Today's
Connection Points

- ***God of Abundance* CD: "Let the Lord/No More Bondage/ Spirit of the Lord (Medley)" (Track 8)**

  As you submit to God and resist the enemy, shout for joy that you are free from bondage!

- **DVD: "Delivered From Bondage" (Chapter 7)**

  Kenneth Copeland proves from Scripture that you have been—once and for all—delivered from the bondage of the enemy.

- ***Prosperity Scriptures* CD (Track 9)**

  Matthew 6:19-21, 25-26, 28, 30, 32-33; Mark 4:20-25, 10:29-30; Luke 6:38, 12:16-21, 32-33, 42-44, 16:10-12; John 10:10, 16:23-24

Faith
in Action

Examine your life for areas where you are giving in to your senses instead of believing what God's Word says.

Make the decision to be moved only by the Word of God!

Notes:

_____

_____

_____

_____

_____

_____

_____

_____

_____

_____

_____

_____

_____

_____

_____

_____

_____

_____

_____

_____

What Are You Going to Do...*Now?*

by Kenneth Copeland

Is it OK for us to just fall apart like everyone else when unexpected things happen? No! It is not OK! It's Gloria's and my desire that you are able to remain strong and steady no matter what kind of unstable atmosphere is around you.

"But, Brother Copeland, how can I keep it together when all of a sudden the company I work for goes broke or lays me off?"

Your very first response should always be, "I'm going to stay in love, stay in faith and do what the Word says and not what I feel!" Then always examine yourself according to 1 Corinthians 11:28, 31-32: "But let a man examine himself.... For if we would judge ourselves, we should not be judged. But when we are judged, we are chastened of the Lord, that we should not be condemned with the world."

Ask yourself, "Lord, did I open the door to this? If I did, I need to know it." Now here's where it gets down deep inside your inner being: "If I did, then I repent with my whole heart, and I am willing to do whatever it takes to fix and change me. Not the boss. Not anyone else. ME!"

So much of the time, after shining the light of the Word on yourself, you come to the conclusion that "if I'd been them, I would have fired me too." Now you've just become stronger in the Lord and in the power of His might. You have just become much more valuable to the plan of God and also to the workplace.

It doesn't matter what "they" think. "They" cannot hold you back. You are redeemed from the curse of anything that the world and its system can do to hold you back. The only thing that holds back and hinders the success of any believer is joining in with that system and doing all the things the world does.

Translated Into God's Economy

Listen, heaven's economy is doing fine, and it's heaven's economy you're tapping in to when you tithe and give and live the principles in this LifeLine kit.

"But I'm living in this world!"

Yes, but you're not under its dominion. The Bible says in Colossians 1:13 that God "hath delivered us from the power of darkness, and hath translated us into the kingdom of his dear Son." To be *translated* means to be taken out of one place and put over into another. In other words, your citizenship is not primarily of this Earth. You are not primarily American or Canadian or Australian, you are first and foremost a citizen of the kingdom of God.

That means this planet doesn't have any right to dictate to you whether your needs are met or not. The Bible says God will meet your needs according to His riches in glory (Philippians 4:19)! The problem is, most believers limit God's blessings by expecting Him to meet their needs according to the meager supplies of this world.

They remind me of a friend of mine who was born and raised in the USSR about the time of World War II. For years all he and his family knew were persecution and scarcity. They lived on the run, first from the Germans, then from the Communists. They ate out of trash cans until they were finally caught and sent to a prison camp.

Eventually, through some miracles of God and the prayers of a couple of grandmothers, they were able to get away and come to the United States. The first place they went when they arrived in this country was a grocery store.

Can you imagine what it was like coming out of a concentration camp and going into an American grocery store? They just walked up and down the aisles of that store and wept for joy at the abundance that was available.

If you would only wake up to the abundance of heaven that's been made available to you, that's how you'd feel too. You'd realize you've been translated out of a world of poverty and into a kingdom that flows with milk and honey.

God's Way or the Highway

The key here is that you must stop trying to do things your own way. There's no such thing as your own way. If it's not God's way, then it's the world's way—where being held back by people, fear, politics, racism, etc., is everyday stuff.

Even if one is a born-again child of God, if he does what causes lack, he will surely have lack. Reacting to loss in anger, fear or self-exaltation, like the world does, only opens the door wider to destruction.

What can we do to grow up and become stronger before these kinds of things happen? Meditate and prepare your mind and emotions to react properly before they happen. That's what God instructed Joshua to do in Joshua 1:7-8:

> Only be thou strong and very courageous, that thou mayest observe to do according to all the law, which Moses my servant commanded thee: turn not from it to the right hand or to the left, that thou mayest prosper whithersoever thou goest. This book of the law shall not depart out of thy mouth; but thou shalt meditate therein day and night, that thou mayest observe to do according to all that is written therein: for then thou shalt make thy way prosperous, and then thou shalt have good success.

Look at the last sentence at the word *observe,* or "see into." "See" yourself responding in love. See yourself never, ever being in lack. See yourself strong and victorious, always with heaven's plan. Don't ever see yourself as a victim. You are victorious in Jesus, always.

"But, Brother Copeland, won't meditating on these things just bring them on me?" Only if you do it in fear. Notice that before God told Joshua to meditate day and night, He told him what to meditate on: "There shall not any man be able to stand before you all the days of your life... (verse 5). Only...." Only—what? "Only be strong and of good courage that you may observe to do according to the Law—My Word, My way! My way is always greater than the enemy's way. Do it My way and prosper. Do it 'their' way and fail."

All this takes time. I know you "don't have time," but you will if you get laid off. Make the time. I don't have time to go back to recurrent flight training twice a year, so I make time. Why? So I don't do something stupid and crash. Take time out of your entertainment. Especially TV. Very quickly, you'll begin enjoying your time in your "life simulator" so much you wouldn't give that time up for anything. Especially after it saves your life a few times and puts you in the right place at the right time.

Evening Reflection

What should be your response when unexpected circumstances happen?

_____
_____
_____
_____
_____

Why are you no longer subject to this world's system?

_____
_____
_____
_____
_____
_____

What are some things you can put aside to spend time in the Word?

_____

_____

_____

_____

_____

_____

_____

_____

_____

Notes:

_____

_____

_____

_____

_____

_____

_____

_____

_____

_____

_____

_____

_____

_____

_____

_____

_____

_____

_____

_____

_____

_____

_____

_____

_____

_____

Today's
Prayer of Faith

Thank You, Father, for delivering me from this world's system of darkness and translating me into the kingdom of Your dear Son. I rebuke the enemy from my life. The devil cannot keep prosperity from me! Lord, thank You that You make my way prosperous and give me success!

Real-Life Testimonies
To Help Build Your Faith

When One Sows, Blessings Overflow!

I have served as the office manager in a local medical practice for 20 years. My bosses—husband-and-wife doctors—surprised me with a dinner to honor my service to the office.

I was awarded a watch valued at approximately $6,000. At the end of the very wonderful dinner, I was blessed with a check for $25,000! We believe with all our hearts that this is a direct result of God's precious favor and what we have learned from KCM about being abundant sowers. We have been so blessed by your teaching regarding this principle. I am excited to see what God will be doing in this year of overflow.

J. & R.S.
Oklahoma

For practical tools to help you get started on a financial plan, go to kcm.org/financial-tools.

Chapter Ten
Your Heavenly Assignment

The Sure Path to Promotion
by Gloria Copeland

You may not realize it, but if you're a born-again believer, you have a quality within you that is in great demand in the world today.

It's a quality employers prize so highly that they'll promote people who have it—and often pay top dollar for it. It's a quality so valuable it can make you a success in every area of your life…including your finances!

What one quality could possibly be so precious?

Faithfulness.

Faithfulness and prosperity go hand in hand.

According to the dictionary, *faithfulness* is "firmly adhering to duty, of true fidelity or loyalty, true allegiance, constant in performance of duties or services." A faithful person is steadfast, dependable and trustworthy. He's consistent.

A faithful person keeps his word. When he says he'll do a job, you can count on him to get it done and done well. He doesn't steal from his employer by wasting his time. He works diligently, even when his boss isn't watching. He's honorable, treating others with the same kindness and integrity with which he would like to be treated.

Spiritually, a faithful person is exactly what that word implies—full of faith. He trusts consistently in the Word of God and acts consistently on that Word. He doesn't have faith in God one moment and doubt Him the next. He steadily believes God and does what He says.

"Certainly, faithfulness is a wonderful quality," you may say. "But I have to be honest, I just don't have it!"

You do if you have made Jesus the Lord of your life and been born again. Because Galatians 5:22 says "the fruit of the Spirit is love, joy, peace, patience, kindness, goodness, *faithfulness,* gentleness and self-control" *(New International Version).* That's the fruit of your reborn spirit.

When you were born again, God re-created your spirit in His own image. He put His own character within you, and one of God's most outstanding character traits is His faithfulness.

As 1 Corinthians 1:9 says, "God is faithful (reliable, trustworthy, and therefore ever true to His promise, and He can be depended on)" *(The Amplified Bible).*

Actually, the kind of faithfulness God has put within us is more than just a character trait. It's a supernatural force that comes to our rescue in times of trouble. It gives us the ability to keep going when things get tough.

The Sure Path to Promotion

Of course, even though the supernatural force of faithfulness is within you, for it to operate in your life, you have to yield to it. You have to develop it and exercise it. But it's worth the effort because the Bible promises that the "faithful man shall abound with blessings" (Proverbs 28:20)!

That holds true in every area of life. When you're faithful spiritually, you abound with spiritual blessings and that opens the door for blessings in every other area. When you're faithful on your job, you abound with financial blessings. When you're faithful at home, you're blessed with a good, strong family.

What's more, Jesus told us that those who would be faithful over little would be made ruler over much (Matthew 25:21). So faithfulness is a sure path to promotion!

Employers, for instance, are desperate for faithful people. The world is full of employees who will just do enough to keep from getting fired. It's full of people who will slack off the moment the boss isn't looking. It's full of people who may come to work—and may not. That's how worldly people are!

But it's a treasure for employers to find a person who works wholeheartedly at his job, who is trustworthy and dependable and honest. So when an employer finds a person like that, he's usually eager to promote him.

The fact is, every believer ought to be that kind of person. Each one of us should live a lifestyle of faithfulness. As Ken says, in every situation we should make it a lifestyle to do what's right, do it because it's right, and do it right. Anything less is disobedience to God's Word.

In the workplace, we should be following the instructions in Colossians 3:22-24:

> Servants, obey in everything those who are your earthly masters, not only when their eyes are on you as pleasers of men, but in simplicity of purpose [with all your heart] because of your reverence for the Lord and as a sincere expression of your devotion to Him. Whatever may be your task, work at it heartily (from the soul), as [something done] for the Lord and not for men, knowing [with all certainty] that it is from the Lord [and not from men] that you will receive the inheritance which is your [real] reward. [The One Whom] you are actually serving [is] the Lord Christ (the Messiah) *(The Amplified Bible).*

Ken and I have seen some of the employees at this ministry take that attitude and, as a result, be promoted again and again. One man started out with the simple job of duplicating tapes for us, but over the years he was so faithful that he eventually became director over the business affairs of the entire ministry.

You may think, *Well, that wouldn't work in my case. My boss is an unfair man. He wouldn't reward my faithfulness.*

That's no problem. The scripture doesn't say your reward will come from your employer. It says your reward will come from the Lord!

You see, God has established a principle of sowing and reaping in the earth—and that principle is always at work. As Galatians 6:7 says, "Be not deceived; God is not mocked: for whatsoever a man soweth, that shall he also reap." If you plant faithfulness in your job, you will receive blessing in return—even if that blessing means a different but better job. Granted that blessing may not come overnight, but if you will not be weary in well doing, in due season you will reap, if you faint not (verse 9).

So make up your mind to put your whole heart into your work, no matter how menial or unpleasant it may seem. Do it well. Do it with a smile and an attitude of enthusiasm and say, "Lord, You know this is not where I want to be. But I am sowing faithfulness into this job as seed for a better job." I guarantee, a better job will soon come along.

Make a Change!

Jesus said, "Who then is a faithful and wise servant, whom his lord hath made ruler over his household, to give them meat in due season? Blessed is that servant, whom his lord when he cometh shall find so doing. Verily I say unto you, That he shall make him ruler over all his goods" (Matthew 24:45-47).

God gives us certain responsibilities in His kingdom. He gives us assignments. Our first assignment might be nothing more than to weed the flower bed at the church or to wait tables at a restaurant. But if we'll be faithful over that assignment, the next assignment He gives us will be bigger and better.

So start being faithful with what God has given you right now. For example, if you're living in a rent house and you want a house of your own, treat that rent house as if it belonged to you. Don't tear it up and be careless with it. For Jesus said, "If ye have not been faithful in that which is another man's, who shall give you that which is your own?" (Luke 16:12).

Before you know it, you'll be among those who "are called, and chosen, and *faithful*" (Revelation 17:14)…and you will be promoted to greater prosperity!

Morning Reflection

What is faithfulness?

_____
_____
_____
_____

How does being faithful lead to promotion?

_____
_____
_____
_____

What assignment has God given you where you can exercise faithfulness today?

_____
_____
_____
_____

Today's Connection Points

- ⦿ *God of Abundance* **CD: "God of Abundance" (Track 9)**

  Worship the One who will be your God of abundance through every assignment you undertake.

- ⦿ **DVD: "God's Peace" (Chapter 8)**

  Receive God's peace as you hear how you can rest in the Lord, even when times are tough.

- ⦿ *Prosperity Scriptures* **CD (Track 10)**

  James 5:1-4; Job 27:13-17; Psalm 37:7-11, 28-29; Proverbs 13:22, 28:8; Ecclesiastes 2:26; Isaiah 60; Haggai 2:7-9; Ephesians 3:20

Faith in Action

Exercise the qualities of faithfulness in your workplace and at home—whether anyone is watching or not. (Jesus is!)

Notes:

_____
_____
_____
_____
_____
_____
_____
_____
_____
_____
_____
_____
_____
_____
_____
_____
_____
_____
_____
_____
_____
_____
_____
_____
_____
_____
_____
_____
_____
_____
_____
_____
_____
_____
_____
_____
_____
_____
_____
_____
_____
_____
_____
_____
_____
_____
_____
_____

What's *Your* Assignment?

by Kenneth Copeland

As you prosper, you'll have great opportunities to give like never before—and here's a word of wisdom to help you be more effective. Don't just scatter your offerings in every direction. Don't sling them at random like grass seed, letting them fall where they may.

Go to God and ask Him to reveal to you where He wants you to focus your giving. Ask Him to reveal to you what ministries you've been especially called and assigned to support, so you can give with greater purpose and power.

I remember one of the first times God gave me a giving assignment. He spoke to me and told me to give $50,000 into Kenneth Hagin Ministries. That was many years ago, when I didn't have $50 to my name—much less $50,000!

"How will I do that, Lord?" I asked.

Don't wait until you have the whole $50,000. Start by giving what you have, He answered. *Then as your harvest comes, give more.*

So I obeyed. I gave the few dollars that I had, then I went to work on that assignment. I sent a portion of every dollar that came through my hands to Kenneth Hagin Ministries. Before long I was completely caught up in it. I had tunnel vision. I was consumed by the vision of giving $50,000 into that ministry.

Then one day the Lord prompted me to call and ask them to total up my giving, so I could see how I was doing on my assignment. Much to my surprise, I found out I had gone beyond the $50,000 mark. I had no idea where I'd gotten all that money. But I did know that I had prospered like never before because I had focused in on what God had instructed me to do.

Of course, when you receive an assignment like that, don't completely stop scattering grass seeds. Keep giving here and there. Bless people wherever you can, but keep the main thrust of your giving trained on your assignment. Let that assignment take hold of your heart until you're just consumed with it. Once that happens, you'll be on your way to the greatest harvest of your life.

Giving to the Poor

One assignment God may give to you is to give to the poor. He admonishes us to do so in His Word—and promises us a return on our investment. Remember that the next time you have an opportunity to buy groceries for someone or help your church's outreach to the poor.

How rich will that return be? Proverbs 28:8 puts it this way: "He that by usury and unjust gain increaseth his substance, he shall gather it for him that will pity the poor."

Considering the interest rates I've seen in my lifetime, I'd say half the financial institutions in the world have increased their substance by usury and unjust gain. So according to the Bible, that money belongs to the Body of Christ.

Until now, we haven't received much of it because we haven't had much pity on the poor. When we did, we've robbed God of the return He wanted to give us by failing to expect Him to bless us as He promised.

I challenge you to give generously to the poor, faithfully trusting God to keep His Word. Give God the opportunity to pour into your hands the treasures wicked men have heaped together for the last days (James 5:3). Let Him begin to bless you with the abundant prosperity you need to help finance the preaching of the gospel to the world.

Investing in the Gospel

Another obvious place to plant an offering is into the gospel itself by investing in the lives and ministries of those who preach the Word. The Apostle Paul gives us clear instruction about that in Galatians 6:6-7: "Let him that is taught in the word communicate unto him that teacheth [or as *The Amplified Bible* says, contribute to his support] in all good things. Be not deceived; God is not mocked: for whatsoever a man soweth, that shall he also reap."

Notice, that scripture didn't say to give to the preachers who cry the loudest and seem to be in the most desperate need. It simply says to give to those who teach you the Word.

We're to give because God says to give, and we're to give as He directs—not because we've been emotionally pressured into it.

Personally, I've resolved never to spend my ministry airtime or my time in the pulpit pleading for money. If this ministry has a crisis, I'll never write you a letter about it. I'll just take my need to God and trust Him to tell you if He wants you to do something to help.

That doesn't mean, however, that I criticize those in the ministry who do ask for money. In part, I understand it. They're concerned that if they don't keep talking about their needs, Christians won't give.

All too often, they're right.

Countless Christians sit around waiting to "feel led" to give to the ministry. If someone gives a tearful, high-pressure plea for money, the "feeling" comes. If not, it doesn't.

But the truth is, God has already commanded us to give, in His written Word. He doesn't say anything about waiting around for some emotional urge. He says we should purpose in our hearts to give (2 Corinthians 9:7). Certainly we must be open to hear God's voice and be led by His Spirit about *where* we should invest our offerings, but we'd be much more apt to hear His voice if we had already determined to be obedient to the Bible and base our giving on His Word instead of our feelings.

Now don't misunderstand. I'm not saying that if you don't give, God's ministers will be left financially stranded. God will always find a way to supply the needs of a minister who is standing in faith. He'll be faithful to keep His promise even if He has to pull that provision out of a fish's mouth or fly it in by ravens.

But that's not how God prefers to prosper His ministers. He prefers to do it through your giving because that way He can bless you in the process.

The best way I know to get rich is to start giving to a minister who has been called by God to do more than he can possibly afford. If you'll do that, God will see to it that you prosper, so He can prosper. He'll bless you with more so you can give more and have an abundance left over, besides!

Don't Miss the Boat

I must warn you. When you set your heart to seek God and ask Him for a giving assignment, you're likely to hear a figure that shocks you as much as that $50,000 figure shocked me. If you do, don't try to reason it out in your head how God can supply you with that kind of money.

Don't try to scale down His instructions and adjust them to your experience by thinking, *Well, God couldn't possibly be asking me for $50,000. That's more than I make in a year. If I gave away $50,000, I wouldn't have anything left to buy groceries!*

GOD NEVER ASKS YOU FOR MORE THAN HE CAN GIVE YOU. And if you're obedient, He'll never leave you poorer than before you gave. He'll always leave you richer.

Evening Reflection

What blessing does God say comes to those who give to the poor?

_____

_____

_____

_____

Why is it important to give to ministries that preach the Word?

_____

_____

_____

_____

What giving assignments do you feel God has for you?

_____
_____
_____
_____

Notes:

_____
_____
_____
_____
_____
_____
_____
_____
_____
_____
_____
_____
_____
_____
_____
_____
_____
_____
_____
_____
_____
_____
_____
_____
_____
_____
_____
_____
_____
_____
_____
_____
_____
_____
_____
_____
_____
_____

Today's  Prayer of Faith

Father God, thank You for putting the force of faithfulness within me. I exercise it today and will be faithful in any small— or big—thing You have for me to do! Show me the assignments You have for me, and give me the wisdom to complete them. In Jesus' Name. Amen.

Real-Life Testimonies
To Help Build Your Faith

The Lord Provides Promotion

Last year my husband was informed that his position at work was being eliminated. We agreed we would speak no negative words. He said that although his position was being eliminated, there *were* jobs of promotion. I told him he must only speak what he wanted to happen. We agreed in prayer for him to be promoted and took Communion, thanking the Lord that He had heard and received our prayer.

We stood in prayer. When he went to interview for a promotion, I wrote scriptures on the job role and told him to pray them before the interview. He enjoyed the interview and got the job!

All glory goes to God. He is so awesome!

K.B.
England

For practical tools to help you get started on a financial plan, go to kcm.org/financial-tools.

In what three areas has your faith grown the most from your use of *all* the LifeLine materials?

1. _____

2. _____

3. _____

What are three ways you are putting your faith into action right now?

1. _____

2. _____

3. _____

As your faith has grown, what are three ways you can be a blessing to others this week?

1. _____

2. _____

3. _____

Appendix A
Prayers and Confessions
Based on God's Word

These can also be found on your Faith in Action Cards.

1. 3 John 2
God wishes above all things that I prosper and be in health—even as my soul prospers!

2. Deuteronomy 8:18
I make it a point to remember, Lord, that *You* give me the power to get wealth—and that's confirmed by Your unbreakable covenant with me.

3. Galatians 3:13-14, 29
Christ has redeemed me from the curse of the law, being made a curse for me. He did this so THE BLESSING of Abraham would come on *me!* I receive the promise of the Spirit through faith because I am Abraham's seed through Jesus, and an heir according to this promise.

4. Malachi 3:10-12
I bring all my tithes—a tenth of my income—into the storehouse. The Lord proves His faithfulness by opening the windows of heaven for me and pouring out a blessing so big that there's not room enough to contain it. The Lord rebukes the devourer for my sake. The enemy will not destroy the fruits of my ground. And all shall call me happy and blessed!

5. Luke 6:38
I give and it shall be given to me, good measure, pressed down, shaken together and running over shall men give into my bosom! With the same measure I give, it will be measured to me.

6. 2 Chronicles 16:9
Lord, I know You are looking to and fro throughout the earth for a receiver. I am ready to receive. Thank You for showing Yourself strong on my behalf, for I am devoted to You!

7. Matthew 6:33
I seek *first* the kingdom of God and His way of doing and being right. I am confident that He will give me all I need!

8. 2 Corinthians 4:13, 18
I have a spirit of faith! I believe Your Word and speak it continually. I don't look at my natural, temporary circumstances, but rather I choose to focus on the unseen, eternal things You have for me!

9. James 4:7
I submit myself—including all my finances—to God. I resist the devil… and he must flee from me!

10. Colossians 3:23-24
Whatever my task, I work at it heartily, as something done for the Lord and not for men. I know with all certainty that the Lord—not men—will reward me. Jesus Christ is the One I serve!

Appendix B
Additional Prosperity Confessions

God wants His people to receive everything He has promised, so knowing what He promised is vital! In addition to the prayers and confessions on your Faith in Action Cards, here are more confessions you can speak as you stand for your financial breakthrough. Remember that God's will is always to prosper His people—He will never forget you nor forsake you!

"To be spoken by mouth three times a day until faith comes, then once a day to maintain faith. If circumstances grow worse, double the dosage. There are no harmful side effects."

—Charles Capps

Galatians 3:13-14;
Deuteronomy 28

Christ has redeemed me from the curse of the law. Christ has redeemed me from poverty; Christ has redeemed me from sickness; Christ has redeemed me from spiritual death.

2 Corinthians 8:9;
Isaiah 53:5-6; John 10:10, 5:24

Jesus has delivered me from poverty and given me wealth. He set me free from sickness and has given me health. He has delivered me from spiritual death and has given me eternal life.

2 Corinthians 9:6-8, 11

With the measure I give out, it is measured back to me. I sow bountifully, therefore I reap bountifully. I give cheerfully and God is able to make all grace (every favor and earthly blessing) come to me in abundance, so that I may always and under all circumstances and whatever the need, be self-sufficient—possessing enough to require no aid or support and furnished in abundance for every good work and charitable donation.... Thus I will be enriched in all things and in every way, so that I can be generous, [and my generosity as it is] administered... will bring forth thanksgiving to God *(The Amplified Bible)*.

Psalm 37:4

I delight myself in the Lord and He gives me the desires of my heart.

Luke 6:38

I have given and it is given to me, good measure, pressed down, shaken together and running over comes back to me—all the time!

Philippians 4:19

I do not lack any good thing, for my God always supplies all my need according to *His* riches in glory by Christ Jesus.

Psalm 23:1;
2 Corinthians 8:9; John 10:10

The Lord is my shepherd and *I do not want* for any good thing, because Jesus was made poor, that I, through His poverty, might have abundance. Jesus came that I might have life and have it more abundantly.

Romans 5:17

I have received the gift of righteousness, therefore, I reign as a king in life by Jesus Christ.

Psalm 35:27; Galatians 3:14

The Lord has pleasure in the prosperity of His servant, and THE BLESSING of Abraham is mine.

Matthew 6:33

I seek first the kingdom of God and His righteousness, so all the other things I need are added to me.

Romans 8:32

God, who did not withhold or spare even His own Son, but gave Him up for me, freely gives me all things .

Hebrews 4:12;
Joshua 1:8; Isaiah 1:19

The powerful, active, living Word of God is always on my lips. I meditate on it day and night that I may observe and do what is written in it. As a result, I am prosperous and successful. And since I'm willing and obedient, I eat the good of the land.

Isaiah 48:17;
Deuteronomy 28:2; Psalm 68:19

The Lord teaches me to profit and leads me by the way I should go. Blessings are coming upon me and overtaking me, as the Lord daily loads me with benefits.

Matthew 21:21-22;
Ephesians 3:20

I have faith and do not doubt. Whatever I ask for in prayer, really believing, I receive from the Lord, who is able to do exceeding abundantly above all that I ask or think.

Matthew 7:7-11

I ask and it is given to me; I seek and find; I knock and the door is opened to me.

2 Corinthians 5:21;
Proverbs 13:22;
Ecclesiastes 2:26

I am the righteousness of God in Christ Jesus. So, the wealth of the sinner, which is laid up for me, is finding its way into my hands. God is giving sinners the task of gathering and storing up wealth to hand it over to me.

Isaiah 45:2-3

The Lord goes before me, levels the mountains and makes the crooked places straight. He gives me the treasures of darkness and hidden riches of secret places. *(The Amplified Bible)*

2 Corinthians 9:10

God gives me seed because I'm a sower. He will multiply the seed I have sown. *(The Amplified Bible)*

3 John 2

I prosper in every way and my body stays well. *(The Amplified Bible)*

Appendix C

Seven Things That Bring Increase

Seven Things That Bring Increase
by Gloria Copeland

The DVD included with this LifeLine kit includes my message on "Seven Things That Bring Increase." The list below is taken from this teaching. These principles are how Ken and I laid a foundation for the prosperous life—and also how we maintain it.

1. **Walking in truth.** This means walking in the light of God's Word, according to His ways, His wisdom and what He says is right. I'm not talking about just reading scriptures about prosperity. You prosper when you have a *lifestyle* of walking in all the words God says to you.

2. **Faithfulness.** Be faithful to continue meditating on the promises in the Word until they overtake your life.

3. **Diligence.** The Word repeatedly says we are to diligently seek God, listen to what He says and obey His commands. Deuteronomy 28:1-2 says when you do, blessings overtake you, because "he is a rewarder of them that diligently seek him" (Hebrews 11:6). And as Proverbs 10:4 says, "The hand of the diligent maketh rich."

4. **Tithing.** Tithing is a covenant transaction that gets God involved in what you are doing. The first 10 percent of your income—the tithe—belongs to God. It's devoted to God, and goes to support ministries that feed you spiritually. Tithing is how you honor God with your money. It makes a way for Him to bless you supernaturally.

5. **Sowing.** After we tithe, we are to sow according to what the Lord lays on our hearts, with the right attitude. The Hebrew word for *offering* comes from a root word that means "to draw nigh." We draw nigh to God with our offering. Second Corinthians 9:6 says: "He which soweth sparingly shall reap also sparingly; and he which soweth bountifully shall reap also bountifully." The Scripture plainly says you reap what you sow (Galatians 6:7). If you desire to be a receiver, you have to be a giver.

6. **Believing.** The Bible says several times, "The just shall live by faith" (Romans 1:17; Galatians 3:11; Hebrews 10:38). Abraham was blessed because he lived by faith. He believed God. We're supposed to live the same way: "So then they which be of faith are blessed with faithful Abraham" (Galatians 3:9).

7. **Saying.** Faith must be in two places—in your heart and in your mouth. "The word is nigh thee, even in thy mouth, and in thy heart: that is, the word of faith, which we preach" (Romans 10:8). Believing in your heart and saying with your mouth produce the operation of faith. Jesus said, "For verily I say unto you, That whosoever shall say unto this mountain, Be thou removed, and be thou cast into the sea; and shall not doubt in his heart, but shall believe that those things which he saith shall come to pass; he shall have whatsoever he saith" (Mark 11:23).

Appendix D

Additional Prosperity Scriptures

Deuteronomy 8:18

But thou shalt remember the Lord thy God: for it is he that giveth thee power to get wealth, that he may establish his covenant which he sware unto thy fathers, as it is this day.

Deuteronomy 28:1-14

And it shall come to pass, if thou shalt hearken diligently unto the voice of the Lord thy God, to observe and to do all his commandments which I command thee this day, that the Lord thy God will set thee on high above all nations of the earth: And all these blessings shall come on thee, and overtake thee, if thou shalt hearken unto the voice of the Lord thy God. Blessed shalt thou be in the city, and blessed shalt thou be in the field. Blessed shall be the fruit of thy body, and the fruit of thy ground, and the fruit of thy cattle, the increase of thy kine, and the flocks of thy sheep. Blessed shall be thy basket and thy store. Blessed shalt thou be when thou comest in, and blessed shalt thou be when thou goest out. The Lord shall cause thine enemies that rise up against thee to be smitten before thy face: they shall come out against thee one way, and flee before thee seven ways. The Lord shall command the blessing upon thee in thy storehouses, and in all that thou settest thine hand unto; and he shall bless thee in the land which the Lord thy God giveth thee. The Lord shall establish thee an holy people unto himself, as he hath sworn unto thee, if thou shalt keep the commandments of the Lord thy God, and walk in his ways. And all people of the earth shall see that thou art called by the name of the Lord; and they shall be afraid of thee. And the Lord shall make thee plenteous in goods, in the fruit of thy body, and in the fruit of thy cattle, and in the fruit of thy ground, in the land which the Lord sware unto thy fathers to give thee. The Lord shall open unto thee his good treasure, the heaven to give the rain unto thy land in his season, and to bless all the work of thine hand: and thou shalt lend unto many nations, and thou shalt not borrow. And the Lord shall make thee the head, and not the tail; and thou shalt be above only, and thou shalt not be beneath; if that thou hearken unto the commandments of the Lord thy God, which I command thee this day, to observe and to do them: And thou shalt not go aside from any of the words which I command thee this day, to the right hand, or to the left, to go after other gods to serve them.

Joshua 1:8

This book of the law shall not depart out of thy mouth; but thou shalt meditate therein day and night, that thou mayest observe to do according to all that is written therein: for then thou shalt make thy way prosperous, and then thou shalt have good success.

2 Chronicles 1:12

Wisdom and knowledge are granted you. And I will give you riches, possessions, honor, and glory, such as none of the kings had before you, and none after you shall have their equal. *(The Amplified Bible)*

2 Chronicles 16:9

For the eyes of the Lord run to and fro throughout the whole earth, to show himself strong in the behalf of them whose heart is perfect toward him.

Psalm 23:1

The Lord is my shepherd; I shall not want.

Psalm 35:27

Let them shout for joy, and be glad, that favour my righteous cause: yea, let them say continually, Let the Lord be magnified, which hath pleasure in the prosperity of his servant.

Psalm 37:4

Delight thyself also in the Lord; and he shall give thee the desires of thine heart.

Psalm 68:19

Blessed be the Lord, who daily loadeth us with benefits, even the God of our salvation.

Psalm 112:1-9

Praise ye the Lord. Blessed is the man that feareth the Lord, that delighteth greatly in his commandments. His seed shall be mighty upon earth: the generation of the upright shall be blessed. Wealth and riches shall be in his house: and his righteousness endureth for ever. Unto the upright there ariseth light in the darkness: he is gracious, and full of compassion, and righteous. A good man showeth favour, and lendeth: he will guide his affairs with discretion. Surely he shall not be moved for ever: the righteous shall be in everlasting remembrance. He shall not be afraid of evil tidings: his heart is fixed, trusting in the Lord. His heart is established, he shall not be afraid, until he see his desire upon his enemies. He hath dispersed, he hath given to the poor; his righteousness endureth for ever; his horn shall be exalted with honour.

Proverbs 13:22

A good man leaveth an inheritance to his children's children: and the wealth of the sinner is laid up for the just.

Ecclesiastes 2:26

For God giveth to a man that is good in his sight wisdom, and knowledge, and joy: but to the sinner he giveth travail, to gather and to heap up, that he may give to him that is good before God.

Isaiah 1:19

If ye be willing and obedient, ye shall eat the good of the land.

Isaiah 45:2-3

I will go before thee, and make the crooked places straight: I will break in pieces the gates of brass, and cut in sunder the bars of iron: And I will give thee the treasures of darkness, and hidden riches of secret places, that thou mayest know that I, the Lord, which call thee by thy name, am the God of Israel.

Isaiah 48:17

Thus saith the Lord, thy Redeemer, the Holy One of Israel; I am the Lord thy God which teacheth thee to profit, which leadeth thee by the way that thou shouldest go.

Jeremiah 29:11

"For I know the plans I have for you," declares the Lord, "plans to prosper you and not to harm you, plans to give you hope and a future" *(New International Version)*.

Malachi 3:10-12

Bring ye all the tithes into the storehouse, that there may be meat in mine house, and prove me now herewith, saith the Lord of hosts, if I will not open you the windows of heaven, and pour you out a blessing, that there shall not be room enough to receive it. And I will rebuke the devourer for your sakes, and he shall not destroy the fruits of your ground; neither shall your vine cast her fruit before the time in the field, saith the Lord of hosts. And all nations shall call you blessed: for ye shall be a delightsome land, saith the Lord of hosts.

Matthew 6:25-26, 28-33

Therefore I say unto you, Take no thought for your life, what ye shall eat, or what ye shall drink; nor yet for your body, what ye shall put on. Is not the life more than meat, and the body than raiment? Behold the fowls of the air: for they sow not, neither do they reap, nor gather into barns; yet your heavenly Father feedeth them. Are ye not much better than they?... And why take ye thought for raiment? Consider the lilies of the field, how they grow; they toil not, neither do they spin: And yet I say unto you, That even Solomon in all his glory was not arrayed like one of these. Wherefore, if God so clothe the grass of the field, which today is, and tomorrow is cast into the oven, shall he not much more clothe you, O ye of little faith? Therefore take no thought, saying, What shall we eat? or, What shall we drink? or, Wherewithal shall we be clothed? (For after all these things do the Gentiles seek:) for your heavenly Father knoweth that ye have need of all these things. But seek ye first the kingdom of God, and his righteousness; and all these things shall be added unto you.

Matthew 7:7-11

Ask, and it shall be given you; seek, and ye shall find; knock, and it shall be opened unto you: For every one that asketh receiveth; and he that seeketh findeth; and to him that knocketh it shall be opened. Or what man is there of you, whom if his son ask bread, will he give him a stone? Or if he ask a fish, will he give him a serpent? If ye then, being evil, know how to give good gifts unto your children, how much more shall your Father which is in heaven give good things to them that ask him?

Matthew 21:21-22

Jesus answered and said unto them, Verily I say unto you, If ye have faith, and doubt not, ye shall not only do this which is done to the fig tree, but also if ye shall say unto this mountain, Be thou removed, and be thou cast into the sea; it shall be done. And all things, whatsoever ye shall ask in prayer, believing, ye shall receive.

Luke 6:38

Give, and it shall be given unto you; good measure, pressed down, and shaken together, and running over, shall men give into your bosom. For with the same measure that ye mete withal it shall be measured to you again.

John 5:24

Verily, verily, I say unto you, He that heareth my word, and believeth on him that sent me, hath everlasting life, and shall not come into condemnation; but is passed from death unto life.

John 10:10

The thief cometh not, but for to steal, and to kill, and to destroy: I am come that they might have life, and that they might have it more abundantly.

Romans 5:17

For if by one man's offence death reigned by one; much more they which receive abundance of grace and of the gift of righteousness shall reign in life by one, Jesus Christ.

Romans 8:32

He that spared not his own Son, but delivered him up for us all, how shall he not with him also freely give us all things?

2 Corinthians 4:13, 18

We having the same spirit of faith, according as it is written, I believed, and therefore have I spoken; we also believe, and therefore speak.... While we look not at the things which are seen, but at the things which are not seen: for the things which are seen are temporal; but the things which are not seen are eternal.

2 Corinthians 5:21

For he hath made him to be sin for us, who knew no sin; that we might be made the righteousness of God in him.

2 Corinthians 8:9

For ye know the grace of our Lord Jesus Christ, that, though he was rich, yet for your sakes he became poor, that ye through his poverty might be rich.

2 Corinthians 9:6-11

But this I say, He which soweth sparingly shall reap also sparingly; and he which soweth bountifully shall reap also bountifully. Every man according as he purposeth in his heart, so let him give; not grudgingly, or of necessity: for God loveth a cheerful giver. And God is able to make all grace abound toward you; that ye, always having all sufficiency in all things, may abound to every good work: (As it is written, He hath dispersed abroad; he hath given to the poor: his righteousness remaineth for ever. Now he that ministereth seed to the sower both minister bread for your food, and multiply your seed sown, and increase the fruits of your righteousness;) being enriched in every thing to all bountifulness, which causeth through us thanksgiving to God.

Galatians 3:13-14

Christ hath redeemed us from the curse of the law, being made a curse for us: for it is written, Cursed is every one that hangeth on a tree: That the blessing of Abraham might come on the Gentiles through Jesus Christ; that we might receive the promise of the Spirit through faith.

Ephesians 3:20

Now unto him that is able to do exceeding abundantly above all that we ask or think, according to the power that worketh in us.

Philippians 4:19

But my God shall supply all your need according to his riches in glory by Christ Jesus.

Colossians 3:23-24

And whatsoever ye do, do it heartily, as to the Lord, and not unto men; knowing that of the Lord ye shall receive the reward of the inheritance: for ye serve the Lord Christ.

Hebrews 4:12

For the word of God is quick, and powerful, and sharper than any twoedged sword, piercing even to the dividing asunder of soul and spirit, and of the joints and marrow, and is a discerner of the thoughts and intents of the heart.

James 4:7

Submit yourselves therefore to God. Resist the devil, and he will flee from you.

3 John 2

Beloved, I wish above all things that thou mayest prosper and be in health, even as thy soul prospereth.

Additional Materials
to Help You Receive Your
Financial Breakthrough

Books

- Blessed Beyond Measure
- Blessed to Be a Blessing
- Build Your Financial Foundation
- Giving and Receiving
- God's Master Plan for Your Life
- Connecting With God's Master Plan
- God's Success Formula
- Go With the Flow
- God's Will Is Prosperity
- Living at the End of Time—A Time of Supernatural Increase
- Living in Heaven's Blessings Now
- Looking for a Receiver
- No Deposit, No Return
- One Word From God Can Change Your Finances
- One Word From God Can Change Your Formula for Success
- Prosperity Promises
- Prosperity: The Choice Is Yours
- The Laws of Prosperity
- True Prosperity

Audio Resources

- From Running Out to Running Over (4-CD series)
- It's Time to Get Out of Debt! How Do I Get Started? (4-CD series)
- It's Time to Get Out of Debt! God Has a Plan (7-CD series)
- It's Time to Get Out of Debt! How to Reap Your Harvest (4-CD series)
- Kingdom Principles (3-CD series)
- Living in Prosperity (8-CD series)
- Living in the Blessing (8-CD series)
- The Kingdom of God—Days of Heaven on Earth (5-CD series)
- The Laws of Prosperity (6-CD series)
- The Blessing: The Power, the Purpose and the Manifestation (6-CD series)
- The Tithe—God's Invitation to Financial Freedom (2-CD set)

Video Resources

- Kingdom Principles (DVD)
- Living in the Blessing (2-DVD set)
- The Blessing: The Power, the Purpose and the Manifestation (2-DVD set)

Prayer for Salvation and Baptism
in the Holy Spirit

Heavenly Father, I come to You in the Name of Jesus. Your Word says, "Whosoever shall call on the name of the Lord shall be saved" (Acts 2:21). I am calling on You. I pray and ask Jesus to come into my heart and be Lord over my life according to Romans 10:9-10: "If thou shalt confess with thy mouth the Lord Jesus, and shalt believe in thine heart that God hath raised him from the dead, thou shalt be saved. For with the heart man believeth unto righteousness; and with the mouth confession is made unto salvation." I do that now. I confess that Jesus is Lord, and I believe in my heart that God raised Him from the dead.

I am now reborn! I am a Christian—a child of Almighty God! I am saved! You also said in Your Word, "If ye then, being evil, know how to give good gifts unto your children: HOW MUCH MORE shall your heavenly Father give the Holy Spirit to them that ask him?" (Luke 11:13). I'm also asking You to fill me with the Holy Spirit. Holy Spirit, rise up within me as I praise God. I fully expect to speak with other tongues as You give me the utterance (Acts 2:4). In Jesus' Name. Amen!

Begin to praise God for filling you with the Holy Spirit. Speak those words and syllables you receive—not in your own language, but the language given to you by the Holy Spirit. You have to use your own voice. God will not force you to speak. Don't be concerned with how it sounds. It is a heavenly language!

Continue with the blessing God has given you and pray in the spirit every day.

You are a born-again, Spirit-filled believer. You'll never be the same!

Find a good church that boldly preaches God's Word and obeys it. Become part of a church family who will love and care for you as you love and care for them.

We need to be connected to each other. It increases our strength in God. It's God's plan for us.

Make it a habit to watch the *Believer's Voice of Victory* television broadcast and become a doer of the Word, who is blessed in his doing (James 1:22-25).

About the Authors

Kenneth and Gloria Copeland are the best-selling authors of more than 60 books. They have also co-authored numerous books including *Family Promises,* the *LifeLine Your 10-Day Spiritual Action Plan* series and *From Faith to Faith—A Daily Guide to Victory.* As founders of Kenneth Copeland Ministries in Fort Worth, Texas, Kenneth and Gloria have been circling the globe with the uncompromised Word of God since 1967, preaching and teaching a lifestyle of victory for every Christian.

Their daily and Sunday *Believer's Voice of Victory* television broadcasts now air on more than 500 stations around the world, and the *Believer's Voice of Victory* magazine is distributed to nearly 600,000 believers worldwide. Kenneth Copeland Ministries' international prison ministry reaches more than 20,000 new inmates every year and receives more than 20,000 pieces of correspondence each month. Their teaching materials can also be found on the World Wide Web. With offices and staff in the United States, Canada, England, Australia, South Africa, Ukraine and Singapore, Kenneth and Gloria's teaching materials—books, magazines, audios and videos—have been translated into at least 26 languages to reach the world with the love of God.

Learn more about Kenneth Copeland Ministries
by visiting our website at **www.kcm.org**

When The LORD first spoke to Kenneth and Gloria Copeland about starting the *Believer's Voice of Victory* magazine...

He said: *This is your seed. Give it to everyone who ever responds to your ministry, and don't ever allow anyone to pay for a subscription!*

For nearly 40 years, it has been the joy of Kenneth Copeland Ministries to bring the good news to believers. Readers enjoy teaching from ministers who write from lives of living contact with God, and testimonies from believers experiencing victory through God's Word in their everyday lives.

Today, the *BVOV* magazine is mailed monthly, bringing encouragement and blessing to believers around the world. Many even use it as a ministry tool, passing it on to others who desire to know Jesus and grow in their faith!

Request your FREE subscription to the *Believer's Voice of Victory* magazine today!

Go to **freevictory.com** to subscribe online, or call us at **1-800-600-7395** (U.S. only) or **+1-817-852-6000**.

We're Here for You!®

Your growth in God's WORD and victory in Jesus are at the very center of our hearts. In every way God has equipped us, we will help you deal with the issues facing you, so you can be the **victorious overcomer** He has planned for you to be.

The mission of Kenneth Copeland Ministries is about all of us growing and going together. Our prayer is that you will take full advantage of all The LORD has given us to share with you.

Wherever you are in the world, you can watch the *Believer's Voice of Victory* broadcast on television (check your local listings), the Internet at kcm.org or on our digital Roku channel.

Our website, **kcm.org,** gives you access to every resource we've developed for your victory. And, you can find contact information for our international offices in Africa, Asia, Australia, Canada, Europe, Ukraine and our headquarters in the United States.

Each office is staffed with devoted men and women, ready to serve and pray with you. You can contact the worldwide office nearest you for assistance, and you can call us for prayer at our U.S. number, +1-817-852-6000, 24 hours every day!

We encourage you to connect with us often and let us be part of your everyday walk of faith!

Jesus Is LORD!

Kenneth & Gloria Copeland

Kenneth and Gloria Copeland